EYEWITNESS ON ALCATRAZ

Interviews with Guards, Families & Prisoners
Who Lived on THE ROCK

EYEWITNESS ON ALCATRAZ

Interviews with Guards, Families & Prisoners
Who Lived on THE ROCK

by
Jolene Babyak

Ariel Vamp Press
Berkeley, California

INTRODUCTION & ACKNOWLEDGMENT

In a collection of critical essays entitled *Under the Sign of Saturn,* Susan Sontag suggested that a written piece, having veracity, emotional power and subtlety, and being written from a system of outrage, should at once sum up and oppose one's age. This has been my goal in writing about Alcatraz and my father's involvement there during one of the most pivotal times of American prison history.

Alcatraz emerged in the 1930s at a time of economic depression, aggressive lawlessness and unchecked media glorification of crime and criminals. The government and the media in 1934 heralded it as *the* escape-proof bastion where only the worst prisoners would be sent, and in which the rules would be so strict as to break mens' spirits. Thereafter official news from Alcatraz was withheld and the only stories to emerge were from ex-prisoners. So the myth of Alcatraz grew. The prison closed 29 years later, an old and decrepit facility, victim of its own myth, discredited by its final escapes and the changing attitudes of prison management.

To claim that it was a brutal prison is too simple. To make a definitive statement about treatment there is reckless, because through the years four wardens ruled, each with vastly different management styles and temperaments, in eras as different as those of Presidents Herbert C. Hoover in the 1930s and John F. Kennedy in the 1960s.

Moreover, it should come as no surprise that many prisoners found when they left that they preferred life on The Rock with one man to a cell and less than 300 prisoners, than to living in populations of 1500, or 3000, or 5000 as in other federal and state penitentiaries.

Therein lies the gray area I've narrated here. My purpose has been to interpret and comment on the statements of the more than 60 people I've interviewed, writing from my own system of outrage, at once summing up and opposing the Alcatraz era. It's an effort, as Sontag also said, to "be true, and not just interesting."

I could have never written this book without a significant amount of work by my father, Arthur M. Dollison, on his own memories of nine years of working on Alcatraz. His sense of history, followthrough and generosity in allowing me to interpret what was ultimately his subject showed more love than I ever knew.

And I would like to thank the following people: Colleen Collins, Operations Supervisor, Rich Weideman, Supervisory Park Ranger, and Rex Norman, Park Ranger, Golden Gate National Recreation Area, National Park Service; Stephen A. Haller, Historian, National Maritime Museum; Irene Stachura, Librarian, J. Porter Shaw Library, National Maritime Museum; John Brunner, who printed many of the photographs; Tom Averill and Jeff Goudie, whose edification, able proofreading and sincere dedication to my project was of immeasureable help; Nan Harper, Tresa Hill, Don Mayberger, Linda "Sam" Haskins, Kathy Hoggard, Marla Eisenberg, Jane Nichols, Tonda Rush, Vickie Randel ; Cirla Dallos, Lacy Curtis-Ward, and Kathy Laurin; Tim Doyle; Rob Wilson, and the gang at BYT; the folks at Negatorium; Miriam Ylvisaker for final proofing; Nancy Olmsted, Ken Fox, and David Bullen; Ruth Teiser, who was a wonderful inspiration to me; and Phil and Ann Dollison whose interest, financial support and love were of invaluable help. *Alas, the errors are mine.*

Please note: The words "convict," "prisoner," and "inmate," all meaning different things to different people, are used interchangeably and do not connote disrespect in any manner. Similarly, the words "guard," and "officer" are also used interchangeably.

Jolene Babyak
July 1990

Library of Congress Catalog Card Number: 88-70100

ISBN 0-9618752-0-8

Cover design by David Bullen
Typeset at Byting Your Time, Berkeley, Calif.
Cover photo and backcover photos courtesy of
   Philip F. Dollison and Corinne Dollison Edwards

Printed by Spilman Printing, Sacramento, Calif.

ARIEL VAMP PRESS
P.O. Box 3496
Berkeley, CA 94703

*. . . dedicated to Art, Larry,
and especially to Evelyn.*

Contents

An armed Alcatraz officer stands on the deck of Tower #2, overlooking the industries area and the yard wall. Little Alcatraz, a small rock visible in low tide, is left of the industries building. (COURTESY OF PHIL DOLLISON)

1

At Last

Prisons are like people. They get old and they break down at the tiniest places. In the final stages of the last escape attempt from Alcatraz, two prisoners cut through bars using string coated with scouring powder. "I got word of it, went up to the armory and checked out a rifle," said Officer Fred Freeman:

[Officer] Pickens and I went out on the catwalk to industries and when we got to about #3 Tower, we spotted Parker. He was on what we call Little Alcatraz, [a small rock off the island]. He hurt his ankle and we kept him pinned down until the boat could pick him up. Every time he'd move we'd fire a round off . . . just to keep him on that rock.

Richard Waszak, who had been an officer on Alcatraz since late 1959, remembers assigning two men:

They had their firearms and I posted [them] on top of Industries. . . I started to head back and one of them started to shoot. They were firing at Little Alcatraz just to get Parker to stay on the rock.

"Boy! They opened fire on that rock. . .That was unreal!" said Mike Pitzer, a teenager at the time. "That was the first time I had been around a prison break where they did any shooting." His father, Edmund Pitzer, had been assigned to Alcatraz only six months earlier, in June 1962. This was their second Alcatraz escape attempt in that time. Mike, his parents, and teenage sister, Doreen, were eating dinner in their island apartment when the escape siren sounded:

I went outside and [saw officers] up on the roof, and they were firing all kinds of shots. I thought they would blow the rock away. They even had two Coast Guard boats on the back side and [the prisoners] wouldn't give up. Then I remember the front guy holding him with a grappling hook and pulling him in.

Dick and Maryanne Waszak had been living on Alcatraz for three years. They had three children, ages two through seven, and the last one was born while they were on the island. Maryanne, a small, thin, vivacious women, who was scared when they moved on—it was their first prison—remembered that siren very well:

*'Course everybody on the island knew you were supposed to bolt your doors, everybody stay in, so the kids were in the house and the doors were locked. We had three doors to the hall [of the apartment building]. And the dining room door was just a flimsy, hollow-core door that wouldn't keep anybody out and it had cracks down the middle. We had a huge bookcase, filled, and it was **hea-vy.** I don't think anybody had ever moved it. And when this went off, 'course he took off and he says, 'Lock the doors.' Well, I did but that door in the dining room's not going to keep anybody out. And there's that huge bookcase and I pushed it in front of the door, and I was a skinny, scrawny little gal at the time. But I got that in front of the door.*

"I know exactly what I was wearing that day," said her husband, Dick Waszak. Although this was his first federal prison assignment, the short, enthusiastic Nebraska man remained in the federal prison service more than 20 years and retired in 1980 as an associate warden:

It was on a Sunday when Scott and Parker went. I had my trousers on and a white undershirt. I'd already taken my shirt off and when the alarm went I reported that way. I remember because [later] I was on the boat—we were out searching the waters—and it was so ungodly cold out there! And of course raining. And that's all I had on.

So went the last escape attempt from Alcatraz. Prisoners John Paul Scott and Darl Parker were discovered missing at 5:40 p.m. on a drizzly, foggy Sunday, only minutes after the last prison count. It was December 16, 1962, (ironically 25 years to the day after the first escape attempt from Alcatraz in which prisoners got off the island).

Alcatraz:
the metaphor for imprisonment. It captured a mythological foothold which linked it with such infamous places as Devil's Island and Siberia.

Although the decision to close Alcatraz had been made earlier that year—a decision fortified by the infamous Morris-Anglin escape attempt seven months earlier in June 1962—the wheels of bureaucracy turned slowly. But with this second attempt that year the island prison would shut down in three months.

It had been a calamitous year for those who lived and worked on the island, and now the federal prison that had generated myth and controversy for 29 years would come finally to an end.

Alcatraz was home to about 70 or 80 kids that year and I was one of them. In any given year about 50 or 60 families and 15-20 bachelors resided on The Rock. Our fathers were the guards, the maintenance men, the lighthouse keepers, the stewards, the industries officials, and the administration officials—the men who worked "up top." Most of us crossed on the boat five times a week to go to school in San Francisco. We played and fought on the concrete parade ground that was our playground. We all had prison stories.

The alleged escape route of John Paul Scott and Darl Parker on December 16, 1962. Parker was found within minutes clinging to a small rock near the island. Scott washed up along the San Francisco shore. Warden Olin G. Blackwell commented that had Scott not washed up, he would have headed towards Hawaii "without benefit of a boat." (NATIONAL MARITIME MUSEUM)

At the top of our unusual neighborhood was a maximum security penitentiary, yet I rarely saw prisoners and paid little attention to them when I did. And parents frequently said they felt safer living on the island than in San Francisco. There was no traffic to worry about, no burglaries to concern us; few of us, in fact, worried about security. Fences and locked gates were everywhere, yet some seldom locked their front doors. Parents were far more concerned one of us might tumble into the bay or fall off the balconies.

There were provocative contrasts. The prison, set so close to the city, was tolerated by San Franciscans perhaps only because it was so silent and fascinating. Merely the name Alcatraz evoked strong emotional images and rather tiresome stereotypes. Because of what they had read, people imagined the worst and questions were constant—sometimes silly: "Do you eat with the prisoners?" someone once asked me. "Aren't you scared?" No, I didn't and no, I wasn't—always.

The film, *Birdman of Alcatraz,* was released while I lived on The Rock, and much of what people imagined came from that good but inaccurate and highly sentimental film. People's concern for the fictionalized Robert Stroud did not match what we knew from our fathers' experiences. Stroud was every inch a character, but he was not the warm, loving character portrayed by actor Burt Lancaster. People vilify criminals, yet sympathize with them when they become prisoners and the public outcry became even more pronounced when a prisoner reached The Rock.

Other ironies existed there as well. Alcatraz was perhaps the most beautiful home I've ever had. On a breezy, crystal-clear day, San Francisco Bay is a magical setting, with two bridges—one, the Golden Gate, perhaps the most famous bridge in the world—defining the perimeters of the cozy European-style city of San Francisco. The bay itself was breath-taking theatre. Ships slid under the Golden Gate past our island; pugged-nosed tug boats churned up the white caps. The waves were frequently dotted with boats and their glistening white, yawning sails. Yet there stood Alcatraz, a mile-and-a-quarter away, a battleship-shaped rock mounted with a three-story, institutional-yellow prison. A flat island mountain lined with barbed wire and guard towers.

It was a peaceful setting, despite all, and perhaps the supreme irony of Alcatraz. We would miss our "poor man's Hawaii" in San Francisco Bay.

We'd miss our 360 degree view of the Bay Area, we'd miss the fog horns that rattled our windows, the island Chirstmas parties, the summer watermelon feasts on the dock. We'd miss the island boat that was always too early or too late to easily catch a movie in the city. We'd miss the shocking, direct current that too often burned out

At the top of our neighborhood was a maximum security penitentiary with cells three tiers high.
(PHIL DOLLISON)

Ironies and contrasts were a part of the setting. Only a mile-and-a-quarter from San Francisco—one of the most beautiful cities in the world—The Rock was a flat island mountain lined with barbed wire and guard towers. Here the Golden Gate Bridge is seen through prison fences. (NATIONAL MARITIME MUSEUM)

TV's or HiFi's. We'd miss the excitement when the escape siren sounded.

"Before the last of us left we took a boat ride around the island," Maryanne Waszak remembered. "We got all the kids, we sat on the front of the boat and I cried and he was crying, the whole bunch of us. It was sad to leave. We were all so close."

That was the feeling we all shared. Although there'd always been scandals, rumors, and even some backbiting among the employees and their families forced to live so close to work, a genuine feeling existed that we were all one family. "If you needed help," said resident LuAnne Freeman, "it was there."

At the end, even we were curious about the Alcatraz cell house, which most of the women and children never saw. "I will never forget right after the last prisoners walked out," said Mike Pitzer:

I went in the cell block. My dad came up and we got to talking and stuff. 'Here is your chance to see what it's like in one of these cells.' And I went in one. There were no personal items in there but everything else was intact. And he slammed the door and left me! It blew my mind! It was something I will never forget as long as I live. . .The doors closed and they went clank and there's a real hollow sound.

An Alcatraz officer opens a cell using gears located at the end of each cell block. (PHIL DOLLISON)

Mike entered the five-by-nine-foot cell, and like a prisoner, he could not see how the cell doors were activated. Gears were located on either side of the cell block, and could be maneuvered to close one or all cell fronts. The levers resemble ones used on cable cars along the streets of San Francisco, and in some ways the sound of cell doors closing is like the sound of a cable car on tracks. But such pleasantries don't remain. What occurs is a drum roll of heavy metal thundering across metal and concrete, as the doors slide into position with a final metal-to-metal collision that echoes throughout the concrete building:

I thought, my God! For the first minute or two, it was like a game, but then I started yelling and I was ready to get out. And there was no answer. I walked up and grabbed hold of the bars thinking I could pull the door open and I couldn't. All you could see was the cell across, and nobody and nothing! . . . That really hit me hard.

About 10 minutes later my dad opened the door. I got kind of weak.

Secrecy surrounded the maximum
security penitentiary, so the
public's curiosity was constant.
(PHOTO BY ROBERT J. HART; COURTESY OF
JOHN BRUNNER)

Security was so strict when the first prisoners arrived in 1934 that the train cars were transported by barge across the bay rather than unloaded on the mainland. Building #64 at the dock, built in 1904-06, stands atop a Civil War-era fort, one of the original buildings on The Rock. (NATIONAL MARITIME MUSEUM)

2

Moving On

Many times I'd hit the gangplank at a dead run. If the tide was high, it tilted only slightly down to the floating platform where the boat was moored.

But if the tide was out, as it was about twice a day, that narrow, pulley-operated, tar-papered gangplank hung vertically and your weight dropped it to the float. Breathless from my run after hearing the boat's whistle, I'd jump down the gangplank, balance on the rolling, heaving float and step across the plumbless deluge onto a pitching and yawing boat.

On nice days I sat outside—ducking the occasional crest of spray at the bow or watching the propellers churn and tickle the sea at the aft. Mostly, however, we were forced inside. Home was only 12 minutes away, but the weather could change from a bright, clear San Francisco to a gray, cold, almost rainy Alcatraz, and seem like a different day.

I usually headed for the cargo hold where my friends were already seated. In 1962 I was a teenager and carrying on a hundred-year-old Alcatraz tradition. School was out and I was going home on the boat.

For 29 years federal prison employees and their families had been catching the daily boat as I had. For 73 years before that—from 1860 until 1933 while it was an Army prison—military families had criss-crossed the bay.

The Johnston family was one of the first to move on in 1933-34. Warden James A. Johnston had been given a rare opportunity to oversee the remodeling of the cell house and island housing during the transfer from military to federal prison.

A 60-year-old man in the prime of his life, Johnston's blue nose polish and doughtiness showed. He had been the twelfth of 13 children in an Irish family, was educated in San Francisco, and by 1919 was admitted to the California bar.

But as early as 1912 he was thrust into the prison business by being made warden of California's vicious Folsom Prison. He was said to have abolished corporal punishment, installed a ventilation system in the cell house, and begun a trustee farm outside the walls in his short time there. The next year he became warden of San Quentin, another vicious "big house." He remained until 1925, abolishing stripes on prison clothing, establishing honor camps, establishing a classification system and spoonfeeding the convicts a little religion. "If we take hate-filled, mentally warped men into prisons and do not earnestly endeavor to correct their wrong notions and replace their anti-social tendencies with finer, saner, and better ideas of their social obligations," he wrote in 1924, a year before leaving San Quentin and becoming a banker in San Francisco, "they may leave prison worse than when they entered, [and] the prison would be a menace to society."

But times had changed and so had Johnston. It was the "dirty 30s," a time of massive unemployment, crime sprees, and well-publicized prison break-outs. In Alcatraz, the government was finally getting its alleged "escape-proof" prison.

Alcatraz was to be the noose over every prisoner in federal and state systems. No man would be sentenced from the courts (although a few were), but would work his way there by recalcitrance in other prisons. There would be no parole directly from Alcatraz either. When a man transferred to The Rock he lost all good time, and had to earn it back before being considered for a transfer out. It would only be by transfer, said "Blackie" Audett later, or "toes up."

Johnston installed new tool-proof cell fronts, added towers and barbed wire around the prison compound and beach. He added new gun galleries inside the cell house, tear gas canisters in the dining room, automatic gun detectors at the dock and at various entrances so prisoners would have to pass through them several times a day. He decided that one guard would serve for every three prisoners (10 or 13 to one was normal), and strictly enforced no unnecessary fraternization among them. There would be no commissary, no radio, no newspapers, no honor system, no trustees. Family visits would be limited and short: one visit a month under two hours. And there would be minimum talking.

The silence would be deafening. And cruel. The rule was eventually modified and abandoned altogether about 1938-39 as unenforceable.

The summer of 1934, as families began moving onto Alcatraz, was the driest and hottest of 70 recorded years in the United States, and one of the most devastating of the Great Depression. Two trains filled with prisoners from Atlanta and Leavenworth penitentiaries snaked their way southwest through the hottest part of the country, moving towards the fog-bound island prison. They arrived on the northern

Alcatraz was a prison for 103 years—from 1860 until 1933 as an Army institution and from 1934 until 1963 as a federal prison.

From the beginning the government intentionally projected an image of Alcatraz as the escape-proof prison. This widely-reprinted photo, with Attorney General Homer Cummings, left, and Warden James A. Johnston inspecting the Alcatraz officer corps, attempted to show the government's determination to deal harshly with depression-era criminals and helped set the escape-proof myth in motion. (NATIONAL MARITIME MUSEUM)

tip of the San Francisco Bay .

Barbara Johnston Ford, the youngest daughter of the warden and the only one to live on the island at the time, was happily unaware of the comings and goings at the nation's most secure prison. She recalls hearing "rumors" that prisoners would arrive by train in August and September 1934.

"Then in August," Esther Faulk, wife of Isaac Faulk and one of the first families on the island, remembered, "the first prisoners arrived, among them Al Capone, you know that?" She laughed. "And the women and children were requested to stay indoors while the prisoners were locked in their cells. . . .Well, we kind'a snuck a look before the boat docked."

Infamous escape artist and train robber Roy Gardner was on one of the trains, as were "Machine Gun" Kelly, Harvey Bailey, Charlie Berta, "Blackie" Audett and about 200 others. But newspapers were mostly concerned about the train they called the "Al Capone Special." The "Chicago Czar" was aboard.

Atlanta Penitentiary hadn't stopped the infamous gangster. It was said he ran his illegal operations from his cell and one prisoner later said he regularly saw convicts with hundred-dollar bills rumored to have been given out by Capone. "Scarface" obviously needed the protection. Years of high living had softened him, and without his henchmen he was worthless as a fighter. His reputation generated bitterness and smirking disrespect.

At Alcatraz he was easily manageable, almost docile. He eventually served most of his 11-year tax evasion sentence there, until it became noticeable that he often seemed dazed and confused. Finally, medical examinations revealed that he had syphilis and he was transferred off the island. He later died in Florida in 1947.

Try as they might, Alcatraz kids squatting behind the balcony railings on #64 building could not recognize the famous Capone when he arrived in 1934. Caroline Weinhold Hoffman, who was 15 at the time, and whose father, Henry Weinhold, would one day be a captain of the guards, was one of the kids below the railing watching the arrival on the dock below.

Mrs. Josephine Michelson, wife of an Alcatraz officer and one of the first families on The Rock, watched from her window. "Our apartment was right up over the dock. . . . I watched the first trainload of prisoners come over from the mainland. They just unhooked the whole train, pushed the cars onto a big [barge] and barged them over."

Alfred Klineschmidt, 14 at the time and among the balcony observers, said, "When they came off, they needed shaves, they were dirty." He vividly remembers the "leg irons and chains running between their legs."

From a distance convicts in chains and four-day beards have a tendency to look alike. But the kids didn't miss the significance of the event, and the camaraderie of being in the center of some larger purpose. The prison had been given a mandate and the parade of convicts had begun.

Islanders quickly saw advantages to their lives on Alcatraz. Children were safely tucked away from busy streets, in a neighborhood where everyone knew everyone else (and everyone's business). The view was breathtaking and particularly momentous at this time because both the Golden Gate and the Bay Bridge were under construction.

The children were fascinated and influenced by the bay. Said Klineschmidt, who later became a career officer in the Navy Reserves, "I could tell every boat that went out the harbor by the whistle. I made it a hobby. I'd write it down, put the pitch on it and stuff— the *S.S. Yale*, the *Ruth Alexander*, the *Mariposa*, the *Lurline*, the *Matson*—I could tell when they were going to sail."

Although the residents were loath to admit it—and still are—they also shared in the notoriety of their impounded neighbors. "Al Capone used to deliver our milk," one well-meaning women said flatly. She was mistaken, but everyone felt some connection. "Mrs. Capone used to ride the boat with us," said George Steere. "His wife. She was a blond and dressed fit to kill, and she always had a chauffeur and body guards with her, but they couldn't get on the boat. She sat by herself all the time."

Capone's ample, Italian mother was also said to have come once, and in going through the metal detector, set off the alarm so many times they asked an officer's wife to search her clothing. Talk among islanders about visitors who came to see prisoners was never malicious, but it was greased by a sense of amused superiority. And it was understood that stories involving famous prisoners were fair game for exaggeration. Mrs. Capone, who barely spoke English, was visibly embarrassed at having to strip down to the metal stays on her corset.

Lieutenant Isaac Faulk, his wife Esther, and their children Herbert, Edward and Ruth outside their Alcatraz cottage. They lived on the island for 19 years. (ESTHER FAULK)

13

Things moved slowly that year, but as more families arrived the social hall became the scene of more and more activities—dinners, parties, games, baby showers, Halloween parties, Christmas gatherings. There was a two-lane bowling alley in the basement, and ping pong and pool tables. Later, there were Alcatraz proms, in which invited "mainlanders" participated, and other entertainment for the teenagers.

But it wasn't the most ideal place to live.

Alcatraz was a battleship-shaped island laid out on three levels. The beach and dock, of course, were the lowest level, and the prison, warden's house, lighthouse and medical technician's house were on the top tier.

Up the long stairs from the dock, however, past the Dock Tower, round the corner of #64 building, passing the island's canteen and post office, down the long balcony overhanging the dock, and up a flight of rock-carved stairs aided usually by a wet and slippery pipe railing, one emerged onto the old Army parade ground where most of the people lived.

Encircling our "big playground" was a small recreation hall and swings and slides, apartment buildings A, B, and C, a duplex usually occupied by the captain's and associate warden's families, and four cottages. The tiny patches of grass that graced the concrete were forbidden to us kids. And although the island was in places lush with ivy, ice plant, blueberry bushes, geraniums, honeysuckle, wild poppies, huge, spiked century plants and numerous eucalyptus trees, most of these were located in restricted areas. Thus, this two-acre slab of concrete was our batting field, our skating rink, our tennis court and touch football gridiron. Just walking across that parade ground could be a bone-chilling experience. Although surrounded by buildings, it was a cement prairie on which the winds played furiously. If the fog were thick, we could walk across it without seeing a single building until within four or five feet of it. Even at night the lights were often shrouded in a thick, pea-soup fog, eerily illuminated by the lighthouse beam as it faded through every five seconds.

"The first thing I remember was the foghorns," Klineschmidt complained good-naturedly, "and the cockroaches the Army left." No one considered Alcatraz altogether safe. Everyone believed in the high-security—it wasn't that. It was the rocks and precipices, the trestles crossing three stories above "Chinatown" to #64 building, the boat rides and dockings, the needle-sharp century plants clinging to the sides of the island, the rocky, treacherous beaches out of sight, out of hearing, and the concrete playground. But the kids didn't care.

"We were hot-shot roller skaters," remembers Joyce Rose Ritz, whose dad, Marshall, was commissary officer the first few years, and helped inmate details paint

About 500 people—prisoners and residents—abided on a 22-acre island.

Alcatraz was a battleship-shaped island laid out in three tiers. Around this two-acre slab of concrete were the residents' living quarters: building #64 rising from the dock at right, the four cottages, the associate warden's/captain's duplex, center bottom, my home for a year, apartment buildings A, B, and C, left, and an officers' recreation hall in the center of the parade ground. Up top is the lighthouse and residence, the warden's house, the medical assistant's quarters, and the prison building. (ART DOLLISON)

many of the "Alcatraz, Warning" signs on the island. "We used to put up a pole and a [sheet] and the wind would catch, and you'd zip across [the parade ground] 30 miles an hour." The winds shot straight from the Golden Gate. "About all the kids broke their bones at one time or another," she said:

We used to climb the rocks around the [prison] workshops, which was fairly dangerous I'm sure. As strict as Warden Johnston was, he was busy putting the prison together, and he wasn't really dealing with the youngsters yet. It was after the place settled down and they realized what we could get into that the rules were set down.

That group of youngsters—about 50 or 60 in all—had more run of the island than any group thereafter, because later more fences separated the prison from us. George Steere lived next to the cellhouse, so kids played up there. Klineschmidt remembers playing football just outside the prison, and on Sundays sneaking up to the building to listen to the convict band.

The danger was there. Convicts stood on the sideboards of pick-up trucks driven by unarmed guards. Some worked in areas where islanders walked, on the dock, for example, where they unloaded cargo from the barges, or on the parade ground where they picked up the trash. But they were never without a guard. Contact between us and them was limited and discouraged, but there were stories of prisoners tossing a ball to a kid, or tipping their hats in greeting. Bill Dolby, a nine-year-old when he moved on with his family in 1944, said he was "sort of" introduced to some of the more friendly dock inmates by the more experienced kids. "There was one they called 'Mickey Mouse,' one 'Popeye,' and there was a 'Donald Duck' too," he said. "We'd talk to 'em, yell at 'em:

One of our major recreations was playing handball and the best thing to play with was a tennis ball that had the fuzz taken off. There were two ways to take the fuzz off. One was to rub it on concrete and the other was to throw it down to the guys on the dock and they'd take it into the shop and buzz it off with a wire power brush. They'd do that for us.

. . .They seemed like average people, they weren't monsters or anything. I can remember asking my dad, 'What did this guy do? What did that guy do?' That kind of diffused any sympathy.

My first mixed recollections of Alcatraz at age seven were the smell of the beautiful, orange starfish that I dried on my windowsill, and at night, the pitch and yaw of convicts on a vocal rampage. (They dragged their cups on the bars and yelled sometimes. Officer Bill Long later said they would often welcome a new prisoner with such a display.) I remember being tucked into bed, asking about the noise, and being reassured that it was just inmates, as we called them, letting off steam. Although my parents never communicated anything as strong as hatred or even dislike for prisoners, I knew instinctively to keep my distance, and that unconscious behavior generated in me a childlike feeling of awe and a hushed reverence, as if prisoners were special people. Special and dangerous perhaps. I found them fascinating—but I kept my distance.

On the windy parade ground in front of #64 building in which they also lived for a time in the 1950s, the author as a child, her sister Corinne Edwards, and their mother Evelyn Dollison. (PHOTO BY PHIL DOLLISON; COURTESY OF CORINNE EDWARDS)

My father, Art Dollison, arrived in San Francisco in 1953 to report to Alcatraz as office manager in the prisons industries. He had been in the federal prison service for 15 years, yet he knew little about the island. Although everyone knew about the city's top tourist attaction, he reminisced years later, "No one knew where to catch the boat:

The people at the hotel didn't know. They told me which bus to take, but the driver didn't know either. He turned in his seat and called out, 'Anybody know where to catch the boat to Alcatraz?'

No one answered, but several looked me over carefully and I shrank a little. I could guess what they were thinking. It wouldn't enter their minds that I could be reporting for work. And since I wasn't an escapee, there was only one possibility: my brother, or son or father was a prisoner.

They weren't sure whether to feel sorry for me, or be scared, and that gave us something in common, because I had mixed feelings about my connection to Alcatraz, and fright and sorrow came out just about even.

Dollison finally found the dock, and after a while the boat pulled in. And although he was recognized by the boat officer, a man with whom he had worked, the officer called the Control Center before letting him board.

We arrived in the spring of 1954 and took up residence in the dismal #64 building. The building itself was like a set from a theatrical show about life in New York City tenements. There were stoops and balconies and fire escapes and bridges over "Chinatown," the dark alley moat where the 1905-06 Army barracks was built atop the original Civil War-era fort.

I had contact with a prisoner once when I was eight. As an officer stood by nodding permission, the inmate handed me one of the favorite possessions on Alcatraz—a black handball that had been hit out of the prison exercise yard. It was a conflict for me whether to say nothing to the inmate, as I had been told, or to mutter a thank you, as I had been taught.

Prisoners had prison names that we heard around the kitchen table, names with stories attached to them, such as the man known as the "Green Lizard," who was rumored to have eaten lizards on a dare, or one called "Suitcase Sally," who, during World War II, allegedly smuggled lead in suitcases, or "Bumpy," or "Porkchops," who was fond of eating them, or "Dog," or "Stubby," or "Creepy" Karpis, or "Jack Rabbit,"

The Alcatraz commemorative postal stamp. (JEAN LONG)

ALCATRAZ
IS SPANISH
FOR PELICAN

ALCATRAZ ISLAND, CALIF.

who was said to have "run like a rabbit" in an escape attempt once. Although the names seemed humorous, and their exploits daring, prisoners often had long, compounded sentences aggravated by incidents in other prisons. Alcatraz was after all "the end of the line."

Some officers and lieutenants kept notebooks to help them get to know prisoners, and no doubt, on a sleepless night, a man might become obsessive about those notes. "Murder-rape-escape," or "42 years, killing," might make an officer wonder why he had brought his family to this. "Life-plus-year-plus-day—murder, rape, escape," might explain why one man went off the deep end, and "good barber," next to a man's name might explain why he got out of D block a little earlier.

Notes like "Death-life-treason," or "ring leader of North Carolina escape," would trail a man from one prison to another and then finally to Alcatraz. "Notorious punk and happy with it—'I got my man'," went one such note about a prison homosexual. "Electrician and good. Also expert lock-picker," went another warning.

"He was a self-mutilator," one officer told me about an Alcatraz prisoner he knew, peering into his notebook and reading, "Five years, life—murder, will screw anything that will slow down."

Consider some of the crimes represented at Alcatraz over the years. One man served a concurrent six years and life for robbery and murder of a custodial officer: while another prisoner held the officer the man slashed him repeatedly with a knife and then beat him with a chair. Another man was serving a 55-year sentence on murder plus killing a prisoner on Alcatraz. He had threatened to kill someone else for spitting on him. Another man had six pages of disciplinary reports at Atlanta Penitentiary, at least 19 of which were serious.

Another man was serving 81 years for shooting into the U.S. Congress. Another man's death sentence had been commuted to life for presiding over a prisoner-of-war camp in which American servicemen were tortured. Of another, serving life plus 21 years for murder, an official wrote, "could let two white men and one Negro out of [D block] if he transferred." (Sometimes prisoners went to D block for protection.)

Although occasionally a man might have commited a simple crime which he later compounded by more serious infractions, such as one on Alcatraz serving "seven years marijuana and escape," more often than not those on Alcatraz had long histories of violence and malfeasance. One convict serving five years for auto theft admitted in court having murdered his foster mother when he was 13 years old. Another serving 20 years for bank robbery and manslaughter had driven a pick into a man's head.

Olin G. Blackwell, who was the last warden on Alcatraz, told me once about a prisoner serving time there. "He explained to me how he killed [a prisoner in another prison]:

He had this piece of brick in a sock and [the guy] was laying on his cot asleep and he whammed him down across the head and he said, 'That blood flew all over the walls and everything.' And he said, 'You shot a hog, haven't you, Mr. Blackwell?' And I said, 'Yes, I've shot a hog.' He said, 'You know how they stick their legs out and kick?' and I said, 'Yeah.' He said, 'That's just the way he did.'

Well now, is that a man you send to Alcatraz?

Everyone knew, as former Alcatraz officer George Gregory once said, "All you have to do is take the bone out of a T-bone steak and you've got an excellent weapon."

The danger was there. It just wasn't obvious. Other than the dockworkers, maintenance details, and the occasional chain of convicts who disembarked from the boat for up top, islanders rarely saw convicts. And our fathers didn't dwell on the subject.

The inconvenience of Alcatraz perhaps concerned us more. In those early days, the boat made only about nine round trips a day, and although the Army boat serving Angel Island stopped at Alcatraz several times, there were wide swathes of time between trips.

But Esther Faulk had a baby when she lived on Alcatraz, the same year eight other women on the island had babies, she said. And she and her husband, later a lieutenant, and their family stayed 19 years. Marvin and Winifred Orr stayed 21 years. The Bergens stayed 16 years. Other families stayed one or two decades, and although they could have moved to San Francisco, few of them did.

Officers inspect laundry for contraband in foreground while the water barge pumps fresh water into the island's fresh water storage tanks and prisoners load laundry and cargo nets into the freight bin. Although water had to be barged, the prison had one of the largest laundries in the federal prison system.
(PHIL DOLLISON)

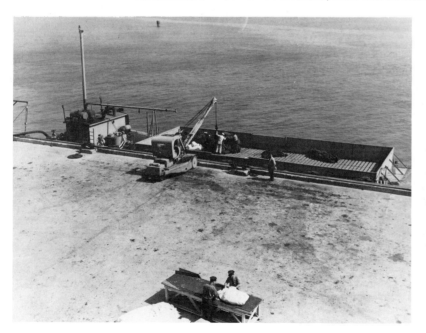

Alcatraz administrators pose as visitors talking through telephones to convicts in this early photograph. Few prisoners received visitors and rarely would four be seated simultaneously. Most convicts were from the midwest or the east and few families would travel such a great distance for one visit a month for under two hours. Throughout the years this restriction was not relaxed. (PHIL DOLLISON)

Tower watch was a long, tedious vigil—an officer stood an eight hour shift for a minimum tour of three months, sometimes six months. Here the Road Tower or Tower #2—manned 24 hours a day—is silhouetted against the faded backdrop of San Francisco. (NATIONAL MARITIME MUSEUM)

3

The Assignment

One Tower was a coal black, octogonal cell with shatter-proof glass. It sat high atop four spider legs and an inner zig-zag staircase that ended at a locked hatch in the deck. Of the six towers it was the principal post, located on the dock and staffed 24 hours a day.

"They shoved you in the dock tower on the morning watch for eight hours and boy that was rough!" said Irving (Levy) Levinson, a small man with a wry sense of humor. "No one to talk to, you don't see a damn thing. And you got to keep your eyes open for the lieutenant!"

Levinson was shot at once during his tower watch.

From here the officer saw the length of the dock, the family quarters in #64 building, the north cell house wall, the yard wall and Kitchen Cage, and beyond to the water tank and Hill Tower. He could not see the industries area, or the Road Tower blocked by the prison directly south of him.

The Road, or #2 Tower, was the second most important peripheral post, and also manned 24 hours a day. Here the San Francisco skyline was to the officer's back. He faced the southeast side of the prison, the yard, its posts, and the yard wall gate through which, during weekdays, a convoy of prisoners walked down the stairs to the industries area. At lunch, and again at about 4:00 p.m., he watched them stroll back to the cell house. He saw the warden's house, the medical technical assistant's house and the lighthouse to the east. He couldn't see the Dock Tower.

The Main Tower, another 24-hour post, sat squat atop the cell house. The Power House Tower, the Hill Tower and the Model Roof Tower were manned only during daylight hours and mostly protected the industries area when convicts were out of their cells.

Two "cages," the Kitchen Cage about 15 feet behind the cell house, manned when the culinary prisoners were out of their cells, and the Dining Room Cage, staffed by the Hill Tower man while prisoners ate, and the yard wall posts, completed the

The Hill Tower, left center, was attached to the prison building and the Model Roof Tower, right, by a long catwalk. Both were staffed during the day when prisoners were out of their cells. At mealtime, the Hill Tower guard walked the catwalk to the Dining Room Cage and stood, armed, outside the building while prisoners ate. The building, left by the smokestack, is the power house, where an old deisel-powered generator pumped direct current electricity around the island.

(PHOTOGRAPH BY ROBERT J. HART; COURTESY OF JOHN BRUNNER)

peripheral security.

Towers were usually three-month rotated tours which could be repeated. They were strictly custody, usually reserved for new officers, sometimes used as punishment, or relegated to those who because of physical or personality factors couldn't work the cell house. Most prison guards, especially new men, pulled tower duty at least once. Almost all men hated it.

As the custodial superstructure, towers were well-fortified:

The guard in the yard wall had a Thompson submachine gun and a .45 calibre pistol [said former Alcatraz captain Phil Bergen]. *All other towers, in addition to those, had a shotgun and a 30.06 Springfield. So they had a shotgun, pistol, rifle and Thompson submachine gun. They also had a gas cartridge gun which could fire both short and long-range gas cartridges.*

Except for a wayward blast from a ship's horn as it skulked into the bay, little distracted the tower officer as he saw past his reflection to the panorama outside. The sun set and the city lights began to twinkle. At night, the Alcatraz lighthouse beam penetrated the darkness with stunning regularity. On clear, moonlit nights, a distant, deep, uneven shadow moved like a front on the water and foretold the freshening of the breezes. Watch officers hiked up their collars, hunched their shoulders and saw the coruscating beauty in the cold and silence.

One of the Dock Tower officers' most important jobs was the boat watch. He kept the key. Everytime the boat was boarded by islanders he clipped the key to a wire that stretched down to the dock, and using a crank pulley moved it down to where the dock lieutenant unfastened it to start the boat.

Former officer Kenneth Bush stands on the #64 building balcony, with the Dock Tower, one of the tallest, free-standing prison towers ever built, in the background.

(COURTESY OF CORINNE EDWARDS)

Each time the boat returned to the island, the boat officer tied the lines, attached the key to the wire, and cranked it back to the tower, then helped the passengers off. The tower day shift saw lots of dock activity; the night shift saw almost none. If this was a normal night, the last boat at midnight and the key exchange would be the most activity Tower #1 saw on his entire eight-hour shift.

"Towers there were very, very monotonous," said Bill Long, a tall, broad-shouldered, expressive man whom convicts called "Big Stoop." "You just sat and looked until your eyeballs hurt."

When the weather was miserable the post was equally miserable. The fog would settle and the foghorns droned, while the watch officers listened for any movement in the gray jungle. Towers had no heat. One man said later that the coldest he'd ever been was one summer when he pulled tower duty on Alcatraz.

The island patrol officer, on the other hand, kept watch by walking the island. His job at night was also repetitive and dreary.

Using his flashlight sparingly, he began his rounds along the beach at the lower east end of the island. If it were a normal night, this was a tedious, silent, naggingly cold vigil. Even on the leeward side of Alcatraz, the damp seeped through the woolen overcoats and dark, double-breasted suits with a vengeance. The patrolman's job was to surprise anyone or anything that trespassed.

"If you ever thought about spooks," said Long, "that was the time to do it." This job also fell to new officers, but they soon learned to distinguish between suspicious sounds and those of surf and seagulls. On more than one occasion, though, an officer skirmished with a yelping sea lion lolling up on the beach, or panicked upon stumbling over a thick, decomposed shark someone had hauled in and left to die.

"We had a real rat problem for awhile," said Phil Bergen. (It was something I hadn't known as a child.)

[In] low tide you could walk out into an area which under normal conditions would be under water. And there would be a lot of stuff down on the beach and all the rats would come down to eat it. . .The rats didn't like to be interfered with and they were big, healthy, mean-looking so-and-sos. I felt that on more than one occasion I was driven off. When you see them in the dark, what you see are those evil little eyes reflected in your flashlight. It looked like a million of them. But of course it wasn't that. Several hundred probably.

Inside, the cell house lid was as tightly screwed on as the glass jars in which we kids used to trap bumble bees.

No carpeting, no wood, no fabrics softened the metal and cement kennel that was the officer's workplace and the prisoner's home. Nothing muffled the noise riveting off walls and shiny cement floors. Nor was the sharp disinfectant smell a comfort, nor the gray and green smoke-dulled paint a welcome sight. Nothing smoothed the hollow, draconian penalty of what was in the 1940s and 50s a maximum security penitentiary.

Entering the main corridor, called "Broadway," 168 cells faced one another. The accumulative sight was awesome; a warehouse of cells three tiers high, stacked beneath skylights that emitted a dull, rheumy light. It looked unnatural. It looked like a human wasp's nest.

Three-hundred-and-thirty-six cells, in three detached blocks—B, C and D—made up the Alcatraz penal colony. (Block A had never been retooled and remained largely unused except for inmate-official conferences.)

For the convict, the day began at 6:30 a.m. Breakfast at 7:00. Works details were racked out at about 8:00 and returned at approximately 11:45 a.m. After lunch, work details were again moved at about 1:00, and returned around 4:00 p.m. (In winter, or on foggy days, industries workers were returned to their cells earlier, or, in some cases, never left their cells.) Supper was scheduled at 4:30 p.m. Lights out at 9:30 p.m. For the prisoner with no work assignment it was an exceptionally long, boring day in his cell. There was little recreation, no rehabilitation, no professional counseling, no television, and little radio.

Boredom and frustration among prison officers also could be a factor. After every major move a prison-wide count was taken. (There were at least 12 scheduled counts a day.) Whether an armed officer walked down from the Hill Tower at meal time to lock himself in the Dining Room Cage outside the building, whether an armed officer was assigned to one of the two gun galleries inside the cell house for eight hours, or whether a guard walked, unarmed, inside the cell house, it was a defensive position. Men had to manage men—a difficult task even among non-criminals. Yet Bureau of Prisons' rules strongly suggested that officers not talk about their work, even to their wives. And to the degree *that* lid was screwed on, made for more tension among officers.

Moreover, Alcatraz was often short-staffed. It needed 110 officers to operate effectively, but often got by with 100 men. Of those, approximately 26-32 were on sick call, annual leave, or their day off, leaving less than 75 officers available to guard

One of the smallest federal prisons, Alcatraz generally held around 264 prisoners.

Except for officers locked inside the gun galleries, no officer who walked among inmates was armed. Officers were forbidden to carry pocket knives, and seldom carried keys to strategic locks. Despite the possibility of danger, few were ever attacked. (PHIL DOLLISON)

250-320 prisoners 24 hours a day. Sometimes lieutenants had barely enough men to cover each position.

This sea of counterveiling tension for both staff and inmates boiled and ebbed constantly. My father sat in a glass office when he was superintendent of industries, an office in the middle of one of the shops with a full view of all surrounding activities. Steadfast to Bureau rules, he didn't talk about his work or prisoners much, but he often spoke of the tension which rose and fell like the tides that lapped against the island.

He could become vaguely aware that a shop seemed suddenly quiet, or that the population in general was withdrawing, and then abruptly, a prisoner could poke his head in the doorway—as happened once—and state that there was a dead man in the laundry, "in case you're interested." Art Dollison looked up sharply. "At least I think he's dead," the prisoner finished calmly.

The kind of man who worked at Alcatraz differed little from men in other federal penitentiaries. The older among them had hired on during the depression. The younger men broke in during the 1950s, at times when work wasn't that plentiful. As a group they differed little from those who entered the postal service, business, or the clergy.

But generally speaking, the older men, only twice removed from the pioneering stock of America, were perhaps a little more gruff, stern, and hard-nosed.

E. J. Miller was a classic example. Miller was associate warden—in those days called deputy warden—under Warden Johnston. While Johnston was the erudite, fatherly role model, Miller was the hammer. On day-to-day matters, Miller was judge and jury.

He was a hot-tempered, pugnacious, thick-skinned, barrel-chested, old-time prison guard. He was by most accounts fair, and described by one kid as "friendly," and "nice." Nonetheless, he displayed characteristics the public per-

(COURTESY OF PHIL DOLLISON)

ceived as warden-like—gruff, scrappy, someone every prisoner liked to best.

"The Dutchman," as former prisoner Dale Stamphill called him, "screamed at the top of his voice and you'd think he was going crazy. But after it was over, that was the end of it. He didn't hold a grudge."

"Miller would come into the cell house and the inmates would boo him, just 'cause they liked 'im," said Marvin Orr, who laughed heartily at the memory. "They wanted to get him mad, see, so they could watch 'im:

One time when [my son] Bob was about eight years old, he picked up the phone and dialed the fire alarm by mistake. That thing went off and Miller picked up the phone, and he starts barking. And Bob drops the phone and runs! [Orr laughed.] *That's how vicious his voice would sound.*

"He was liked and he was feared and he was hated, all rolled in one," said former Alcatraz prisoner, Clarence Carnes. Cons called him "Jughead," and "Meathead," a typical derisive con name, and several men remembered an incident when Miller became furious because a new arrival accidentally called him "Mr. Meathead."

Miller was legendary for cussing out anyone who crossed him at the wrong moment, but he also related to prisoners easily. He liked to make bets with them, using "hole time" as the wager. Benjamin Rayborn, a former Alcatraz prisoner who later became successful as a law researcher for the San Diego Federal Defenders Project, said that Miller loved the St. Louis Cardinals:

If you said you thought the Dodgers would beat the Cardinals and won, you got out [of the hole].   He'd make another bet. 'I'm out now,' you'd say. 'That's alright, you'll be back!   We'll count it on the next time.'

The kind of man who took the job and liked it was often a man who found interaction with prisoners to be fascinating.

A dry, droll sense of humor helped. "Greatest stories in the world," said George Gregory, an Alcatraz federal employee for many years.

Gregory was a Marine who was injured during World War II. The prison service, for which he'd worked before, helped him throughout his year-long recovery, then took him back. In late 1946 he transferred to Alcatraz.

He was a bachelor, a rare bird on an island where most were married. He played the role to an amused female audience and a slightly concerned male audience, but eventually married and settled north of San Francisco. During the 50s, however, he turned down promotions to other prisons because, he said, he liked the Bay Area. He was a junior officer, and sometimes made acting lieutenant, skipping over other senior officers, who would resent it. He sometimes remained acting lieutenant for months at a time, and groused that it was a good way to get a lieutenant's responsibilities on a junior officer's pay. "At least 70 percent of the persons who work in prisons shouldn't be there," he scoffed, "and they'd probably say the same about me."

"Convicts were pretty proud of their caps," he began, remembering the blue-gray railroad caps they wore:

*And one time a guy's hat gets drop-bombed by a sea gull. And another con says, 'Wait—I'll get some toilet paper.' After he leaves another convict says to the first guy, 'How dumb can **he** be? By the time he gets back with toilet paper, that sea gull'll be long gone.'*

Ten Alcatraz officers pose in 1953. Over the years the guard's uniform resembled a policeman's uniform less and less (see page 11 for comparison), until in the 1970s a blazer and slacks became more common. Only two officers have been identified, Captain Emil Rychner, bottom left, and Deane Dorsey, lower right.
(COURTESY OF HAZEL DORSEY ANDERSON)

Gregory wasn't as hot-tempered as Miller, and by no means in the same category, yet he wasn't afraid to diffuse the sting of such a man with his biting humor. Warden Edwin Swope was another old-time prison man whom prisoners loved to hate. Warden from 1948 until 1955, Swope was well known for riding roughshod over his officers, pitting one man against another and plummeting morale in his wake. He was a perplexing man to be at the helm of the nation's tightest security penitentiary and there were many stories about him.

Several officers remembered that when he moved off the island in 1955 he assigned prisoners to move his belongings to the island truck for passage to the dock. Gregory was at the truck when one inmate came out of the warden's house carrying his shotgun.

He had a dog, something I and every kid on the island remembered during those years. (Islanders weren't allowed dogs or cats.) Whenever Bureau officials came on the island, Swope dispatched a guard to hide the dog on the mainland for a while.

He also habitually put his arm around whoever he was talking to—officers and prisoners alike—calling him "M'boy," in a friendly, condescending fashion that many disliked. He did it once to Gregory. Gregory pulled his arm away, then deliberately examined his hand for a moment, until Swope asked him what was the matter.

Gregory mused, "I just wanted to see if there was a knife in it."

The men who arrived later to become federal prison officers were of a different generation. They resembled the businessmen of the 1950s. They felt men like Miller and Swope were too hard-nosed and unenlightened. They sometimes regarded men they worked with as little better. When asked casually what was the difference between inmates and officers, former Alcatraz Medical Technical Assistant Tom Reeves remarked cynically, "There's more sociopaths among the prisoners."

An officer, left, checks the daily roster while inmates move to their assignments. "Convicts," George Gregory said, "had the greatest stories in the world." (PHIL DOLLISON)

Although a wry generality, the remark is no overstatement. There's no denying the dynamics of imprisonment: one group of men is guarding another. Within that obvious framework lies an undercurrent of suspicion and emotional turmoil.

Alcatraz, like all prisons, contained a limited population with a lowered cultural level; basic convict intelligence was nearly that of the general public but convicts were undereducated by about four grade school years. Between 15 and 20 percent were emotionally disturbed, ranging from complex neurotics to psychotics. Most were poor even in vocational skills. The group as a whole was unstable and uncohesive, participation in criminal activity being the basic common characteristic. Short tempers and frustrations provoked quick anger that had a compounding effect on their situation. Convicts were transferred in and out for custodial reasons; making friends was fraught with acute emotional needs and challenges.

Particularly at Alcatraz there was widespread ignorance of events, news, and time, keeping prisoners at a distance from the real world and fostering a demoralizing feeling that no one outside cared.

Fights, sexual attractions, triangles, misunderstandings and manipulations ebbed and flowed constantly at Alcatraz, probably because of the extreme boredom. Prisoners often found themselves in scrapes that sometimes lost them their jobs, their friendships, or their self-respect. They often wrote letters to try to explain their circumstances. The letters were very conciliatory. "Mr. Donaldson: Please excuse the liberty I take in writing you this letter but I was wondering if you were going to give me the back Pay for running the 2 mechines [sic] since April. . ." wrote one prisoner to Art Dollison. The tack seemed to be one of pleas, conciliation, bargaining and hope, the victim trying to obtain some bit of fairness. "I am sorry to write you a letter of this sort. Please believe . . ." wrote another prisoner about another incident.

". . . Please believe: I am disgusted with myself for my part in the fracas and promise you I will make the greatest possible effort to negate a recurrent . . ." wrote a man to both the warden and the superintendent. Such letters often contained promises: "If I am guilty of any of the foregoing I am to consider my job to be a forfeit . . ."

Such unmasked, cloying humility seldom elicited the desired effect. Not when the most common type of communication from a guard was a command, and the most common refrain from a prisoner was a question. Moreover, the expressed humility was at odds with the pervasive violence. A vast cauldron of felt and real injustices boiled, and prisoners had an excess of time to stew, scheme and connive. In such a situation, ridicule, smirking insolence, heavy sarcasm, withering, domineering mockery and contempt were normal reactions among prisoners.

"Popularity was power in prison," said Clarence Carnes. "Other prisoners didn't touch you if you had friends."

33

Among guards, although few characteristics determine who becomes one, the subliminal conditioning *after* a man takes the job is difficult to avoid, and is expressed in increasingly ironic and paradoxical ways. This is especially true in any maximum security penitentiary. In talking about Alcatraz officers' attitudes, one old-timer and former officer said, "They thought those [prisoners] were *animals* and most of them were." Everyone who'd ever been in a max pen knew there was some truth to that, but few would say how much officers contributed to it by their own attitudes.

Some men were far more obvious about their feelings for the "degenerates," "homos," and other "undesirables" they guarded. "Some of them guards," said one Alcatraz officer, "didn't like niggers." It was one man's revealing statement.

And although most prison men aren't prejudiced, hateful, or mean-spirited, the interaction between officer and prisoner is at best a flawed one.

Guards are the enemy, yet relationships among prisoners were far more punitive than relationships between prisoners and guards.

Most assaults in any given year were prisoner-upon-prisoner. Thirty-three assaults occurred on Alcatraz in 1958, for example, as listed in a year-end report to Washington. Of those, 29 were inmate-on-inmate. Most were fistfights, but some prisoners used knives, a metal pipe, a trumpet, a chair, or an iron weight.

Phil Bergen, Captain of the Guards 1949-55. (PHIL DOLLISON)

"They were always ready," said Phil Bergen, "and when some little thing happened, it'd just turn 'em loose." Bergen worked on Alcatraz from September 1939 until June 1955, living on the island with his wife and two daughters. He became captain of the guards in 1949, and it was in this position that I met him as a child. As captain, he was tough, unassailable and respected—but not always liked. "Here lies Bergen under the grass," remembered one interviewee who saw the epithet written on an Alcatraz wall, "now the maggots can kiss his ass." Walking to his home on the parade ground after work in his dark uniform, his captain's hat hitched low over his eyes, he looked every bit the frightening, gruff man whose reputation preceded him. But years later when I knew him as an adult, I found him intelligent, thoughtful, and occasionally convinced by a well-reasoned argument. Although well into his 80s, he was going strong and had become a spokesman on Alcatraz, which earned him even more jealousy from other former officers.

"I never struck the first blow or called them any obscene names," he said in a broadcast once about prisoners. His approach was simple and somewhat survivalist. "On the other hand, if a prisoner struck me, I never could entertain this idea of merely trying to restrain them. If I were struck, I struck back. And tried to strike back a little harder." Bergen saw it sometimes as a game to be played out:

They had a great big iron basket that was made in the shops [he said, in speaking of how inmates would get back at the guards]. *And they hung that on the end of the sewer pipe [down at the bay].   Every once and a while the inmates would flush their clothes down the toilet. . .On one of the days when they were mad for some reason, you'd expect a general flushing of clothing. We'd take an [inmate] detail down and they'd pick all that crummy clothing out of the basket and take it back to the laundry and launder 'em and give it back to 'em.* [He laughed heartily.]   *It's crazy, isn't it?*

"You didn't go around hollering at them, 'Heh! You! This!'" said Bill Long. "They knew you got authority, so they're not going to fight. But if you go around and show your ass, then you're going to struggle all the way."

"You don't get cooperation out of a guy who hates your guts," said Isaac Faulk in speaking of the public's misconception about prison officers. Most men soon learned to ignore petty infractions. If you were a guard who purposely messed up a con's good time, he resented it, and worse, he'd talk it up among his buddies. "And they're more organized than the guards are," Faulk said.

"I had inmates over the years working for me that I put more trust and confidence in than I did some of my fellow officers," said Marvin Orr, who worked there from 1939 until he retired in 1960. He recounted a story of one prisoner who actually jumped in front of another convict who threatened Orr with bodily harm. " 'You get Orr after you get me'," he said the prisoner said.

Orr's story is not that unusual. A small, wiry man, with a face as deeply lined as a cracked river bed, Orr settled in the Bay Area after he retired from Alcatraz, and he befriended several convicts after leaving prison. When one man died, Orr and his wife went to his funeral, having known the man for many years.

Even in that regard Marvin Orr wasn't that unique.

"I'd even take some of these old thugs—when I was up in Leavenworth—and bring 'em home and feed 'em," said Bud Mawbrey, former Alcatraz officer. Mawbrey (not his real name) had been in the Marines during World War II, and had earned the Navy Cross for heroism. That gave him a taste for being where the action was, and once the state-side Marines lost its excitement, he joined the prison service and served on Alcatraz from 1947 until 1960. He was a large, fearless man, described by one as a "damn good prison man," by others as intimidating and blustery. "Get permission from the warden and bring 'em home," he continued:

An unknown Alcatraz prisoner humorously depicts glove shop supervisor Al Larmey as a convict. (COURTESY OF ART DOLLISON)

36 Alcatraz prisoners were often said to have had the best food in the federal prison system on the theory that well-fed men wouldn't fight nor attempt escape. (PHIL DOLLISON)

The dining room in any prison is considered one of the more dangerous places for an unarmed guard. This photo dates from the later years at Alcatraz when four-man tables and tablecloths were used. Note the musicians in the background— it was probably a holiday. (COURTESY OF PHIL DOLLISON)

I used to take 'em out and run 'em around town. Never been outside the institution in 30 years! I figured they wasn't going to do nothing I couldn't handle. I took one feller, John Paul Chase, home for dinner. . .I'd known him for 20 years. [Florence Madigan Stewart said that Mawbrey brought Chase to their home one night.]

"You get a rapport with convicts," Geroge Gregory said matter-of-factly. Gregory, whose cynicism and battle experiences often matched those of prisoners, established rapport through humor and a pragmatic realism. "And you don't ever tell a lie, see. They're allowed to tell lies—that's part of the game. But you're breaking the rules if you lie."

"When I was coming up on the island," said Phil Dollison, "I never saw any tension between guards and prisoners. I saw lots of inmates and guards working together, but I never saw anyone being disrespectful, or condescended to, or yelled at. The public consensus was that Alcatraz was a brutal prison, but it wasn't; the prisoners ate the same food as the guards, they were always clean, they looked sharp, and everyone was always respectful of one other."

It was the smart officer who treated prisoners fairly. "Either [prisoners] respected you or they did not," said Bob Fawson, who worked on The Rock from 1958 until it closed in 1963. [Fawson was interviewed with the agreement that his real name not be used.]

. . . If you were known as a guy who—in order to get back at an inmate—would bum-rap him or plant something on him, God help you if the inmates ever took over the cell house.

Brutality is a more highly charged word than violence. And if you ask was there brutality at Alcatraz the answer would be yes.

But there's a hitch that often sociologists and the public forget: prison brutality is double-sided, moving in an always escalating retaliation. One provokes another. The reasons for the escalation are as common as the tension.

"There could be a killing," said former prisoner Clarence "Joe" Carnes, "and it could happen so easily—over nothing." He snapped his fingers for emphasis. "I have **seen** these nothing things happen!" Carnes served at Alcatraz for 18 years and was one of the youngest men ever sent there. He was a naive, gullible, boyish Choctaw

Indian from a dirt-poor family in Oklahoma. Truancies and penny-ante stealing during the depression led eventually to robbery of a gas station with a partner. Gun in hand, the robbers shot and killed the attendant. With no previous arrests, he said, he pled guilty and received a life sentence.

At Oklahoma State Reformatory in 1943, he ditched a rock quarry crew, ran away, coerced a driver to cross state lines, and got charged with what convicts call "technical kidnapping." Carnes later said he went three blocks and got five years. But that wasn't all: he pled guilty and got 99 years for the kidnapping and five years for escape. He was sent to Leavenworth, then quickly to Alcatraz. He arrived in 1945, a bitter, sullen, silent Indian with a chip on his shoulder. He was 19 years old, and a year later, participation in another escape attempt earned him another life sentence. He didn't leave Alcatraz until it closed in 1963. When we met in 1979, out of prison, he was a sincere, thoughtful man who had lost his bitterness, and who took responsibility for his poorly played-out life. "Words just flare up," he said:

It could be a domino game or an argument on the handball court as to whether the ball is out. . .The method of dealing throughout their lives has been violence, so that's what they resort to.

. . .The thing where they drew straws on the yard, [he said of another incident in the late 50s when convicts decided who would kill another, hated con]. *And then saw it through. He was knifed but he lived. . .It symbolized the viciousness, the deadliness that you walked with all the time. . .The cold thing about it is that Alcatraz had fewer people like that than any other major institution in the country. So you can picture what these other prisons are like.*

"Outside, if you see someone being hurt," said Henry Floyd Brown in the visiting room at Kansas State Penitentiary in 1983 (Brown was at Alcatraz

D block was also stacked three tiers high. The regular cells above were larger. Of the 14 floor cells, six had gate fronts as well as solid doors which would leave someone in to-toal darkness and silence. These were known as "the hole." (PHOTO BY PHIL DOLLISON)

for three years in the early 50s), "it's just normal procedure to call the police.   In prison, if you see a guy laying on the tier with his throat cut, why, you walk on by and ignore him.   Because you don't know why he was killed and **_he might'a needed killin'._**"

Most brutality in prison is between inmates. Actual retaliation between officers and prisoners took on a less deadly but more humiliating tendancy. Convicts could retaliate by shredding an officer's uniform, or their family's clothes in the laundry. "They'd razor blade the hell out of some of that stuff," Carnes said later.

But there were more degrading ways. "Guys in the hole from time to time," he began, "might give the officers a hard time:

> *And after all, there would almost always be someone down there who was a hardass.   Now I did this myself: take a shit and piss in the toilet and made a goo of it and put it in a paper cup [we] were allowed to drink with, and when the lieutenant opened the door, poured it right in his face. Me and Porkchop and K. was on a hunger strike. And we got mad one night. So they took our blankets. So when the lieutenant opened the door at 3:00 a.m. we hit him. He said, 'What have I done to you?' And K. said, 'Get the son-of-a-bitch again!' And he slammed the door and went. But they didn't do anything. I've seen them beat guys up that did that.*

In fact, fights between prisoners and officers occurred most often because of D block. Also called the Treatment Unit, or TU, D block contained the cells variously called the "segregation," "isolation," "solitary," "dark," or "hole" cells. D block was walled off from the main population; men there did not eat or go to the yard with the others.   Some stayed for years, having murdered a prisoner or guard, or having been involved in an escape attempt or caught in a violent, homosexual triangle.   Others earned segregation for a shorter time, depending on the severity of their deed. Still others netted the Special Treatment Unit, or the "hole," the six dark cells, which, when fully closed, formed an isolation tank. One fought his way to the hole by decking an officer or by violent, repeated outbursts of anger. Hole time, according to Art Dollison, could last from one to 30 days.

"A lot of times a prisoner don't want to go to the hole, see, and especially if he's mad," said former Lieutenant Faulk. "So you have to use force to do it."

"If they don't come out, " said another officer, "we go and get 'em.   That's part of the job you signed on for."

It was possible for a man to go from one of the most lenient institutions to Alcatraz in a short time. One man did; first confined at the National Training School for Boys, he quickly progressed to Chillicothe, then Terre Haute, Lewisburg and Leavenworth—increasingly secure prisons— until he wound up at Alcatraz, serving for a time in the hole. He was 22 years old.

The underdog, the convict, was usually the first to throw a fist. That he'd get slugged or beaten up because of it was a consequence he knew was probable; that he'd get thrown in the hole, especially if he continued to resist physically, was probable. He knew that if the next time an officer approached his cell he continued his vituperative outbursts, it would earn him tighter lock-up. Not only the grill front but the solid door would shut, leaving him in total eclipse, isolated with just his own thoughts and sense deprivation. Further humiliation was possible, but it usually rested on the behavior of the inmate. Nonetheless, this is where the circumstance of prison violence and and the charge of brutality to prisoners becomes cloudy.

"Some guards would probably be apprehensive," Clarence Carnes said:

Everybody there was probably doing so much time and on any given day he night decide to die. The officers were aware that they could only push you so far. It wouldn't be wise to come down on you very hard. They dealt with situations intelligently and unemotionally for the most part. . .That might be the reason why in all the years I was there they never beat me, never kicked me, because I was doing so much time. . .I just might decide to die— commit suicide—take somebody with me.

But officers did talk guardedly of unnecessary violence. Bill Long recounted an event that occurred one Christmas during his years at Alcatraz:

Clarence Carnes, prisoner on Alcatraz from 1945 until 1963.

I think it was breakfast, and pretty soon I looked up and the damn Christmas tree was going back though the mess hall. [Christmas was a difficult time for some prisoners; in this case the man was tired of looking at the tree, he later said, and he wanted it down.] *Well . . . about three officers grabbed him and about that time you heard this 'pop-pop-pop' and that was one of your gentlemen with the sap. [The] lieutenant was raining this guy's skull with about three or four shots with the sap, and—ah—the inmates really got up in arms about that. We're holding the guy by the arms and he's laying sap on him.*

But other incidents were even less clear. "There was a man in a solitary cell, and he was using excrement, and every time the officer opened the door he'd throw it at the officer," Bud Mawbrey told me:

His cell was filthy, stinking, it was unsanitary. He used his excrement to mark the walls. So we went in to move him, to put him in a clean cell and give him a bath, and he resisted us. . .We had to control him. And there's only one way to control him, that's to knock him out.

Otherwise there was three of us, and you're trying to hold a slimy guy covered with crap, and take him down and shower him, and you just can't fight him all the way. The best way is to put him out, put him in the shower, bathe him, put him in a clean cell and when he wakes up, didn't hurt him. Boxer don't get hurt when he gets knocked out. But ah, the Bureau don't like that. They frown on that . . .

Prison men judge each other by their willingness or unwillingness to take part in such confrontations. The tougher guards were disdainful of the majority of men who, as Bergen put it, would "fade away" when a fight ensued. The men who avoided fights were contemptuous of the small "goon squad" that existed to handle the rougher residents. But in a dangerous situation they called on those men to help out.

It was a duplicitous arrangement that caused some officers to feel betrayed by their colleagues in the end. "Every time they had trouble in a unit at Alcatraz, they'd say, 'Go get Mawbrey.' So I was in on it, see?" Mawbrey said somewhat bitterly. "What'd they say [in the end]? 'Well, he's just an old thug'."

But perhaps men judged each other less by the force they sometimes administered than by the relish they displayed in administering it. "There was no brutality at Alcatraz," an officer would say disdainfully. "Some of them got brutal in there," another would counter. So it sometimes goes in a maximum security prison, especially when a warden doesn't always know—*or want to exactly know*—how officers handle prisoners.

But guards, said one prisoner, were *insane* about security, and shivs were the principal reason. Knives made out of tableware, nail files, shanks of steel, halves of scissors, pen parts, screwdrivers; knives with three and four-inch blades filed razor sharp; knives with foot-long blades were the reason men were insane about security. Lives depended on it.

"I always started at the top," said George Gregory, who after the inmate orderlies were released (they waxed and buffed the floors, painted cells and made minor repairs), would fulfill a lieutenant's order to shake down cells:

"Sap's got a handle-like, and it's got a spring in the handle, and it's got buckshot or a piece of lead," said one officer. "The big reason they never said nothin' about 'em is because they was far less harmful than using a wooden billy or one of those gas billies."

I would take the books, rifle through them, 'cause they can often cut the pages out of the inside and hide things in there. And then I'd go through their clothing, me-tic-u-lous-ly. Then their bed of course. And also some beds had hollow legs and you had to check on that because they could put stuff up [there]. And shake every blanket down, and to the best you can, you'd check the mattress, especially check for rips or a new sewing job. And also, we'd periodically take the mattress out and run 'em through a metal detector, and change mattresses.

And the little air vent at the bottom [of the cell]?—check that to see if there's any strings hanging down, where they might have something tied on . . .

Left: In the early years prisoners were permitted very few items in their cells and each item was noted by the cell house officer in charge. Although security was always an issue, in later years lieutenants felt the pressure to be more relaxed in permitting many more items in cells. (NATIONAL MARITIME MUSEUM)

Right: Prisoners were allowed to change cells and some did frequently, to avoid someone, to be near a friend, or because of security reasons. (PHIL DOLLISON)

Five Alcatraz children (including the author as a child, right) stand before a fenced-in playground 1955. Parents worried about their children more with regards to the beaches, rock precipices and concrete playground than to prison security. "Billy'd be down at the beach and back before you'd know it," said Jean Long of her 10-year-old. (PHOTO BY CORINNE EDWARDS)

4

Life on the Rock

It was just like ants when the school boat whistle blew. Kids ran out of their apartments, across the big playground, down the steps by the side of #64 building and through the balcony; they plowed down the steep, terraced, concrete stairway between the balcony and the Dock Tower, hitting the dock about the same time the boarding whistle blew.

Most of us got pretty good at bouncing down those steps two and three at a time, while a silent and rather stern woman known as the "balcony lieutenant" watched daily from the railing of #64 to make sure none of us fell into the bay.

Bill Dolby, who was nine years old when he moved on the island in the 1940s, used to wait until the last minute to run for the boat. "I was always cutting it close, so was my mother," he said. "The whistle would blow and that would be about the time we would dash out the door. I had those steps down pat and I could go down about six or seven at a time, full speed. I never fell, but I'd be the last on the boat, time after time."

Our lives were punctuated by the boat schedule, and the comings and goings of the broad-beamed, high-bowed cruiser, the *Warden Madigan,* an old Korean War off-shore island steel supply boat converted for use at Alcatraz. In the last days of Alcatraz the little launch made 22 round trips a day. The school boat was the 7:10 a.m. and by 3:30 or 4:10 p.m., we were back for the 12-minute ride home.

Dick Waszak was the boat lineman for awhile. His job, once the boat pulled into the dock, was to grab the line connected to the pier, tie up the boat and assist everyone in boarding. Waszak learned quickly that his was not always an easy task. "The lines? Yeah, [they] pulled me into the water and almost killed me there," he said:

We had already reached Fort Mason [where the boat later docked on the *mainland]. The seas were real rough. I reached out with the gaff to get ahold of the line and the boat went one way and the line went the other. I held onto the line . . . and dropped between the boat and the float.*

"You have to understand," said Pat Mahoney, an Alcatraz officer who was the licensed boat operator for nearly four years in his six years on Alcatraz, "in those swells [a boat] can almost drop four feet. And Waszak was a very determined individual. He held onto that line. Well, it should have killed him."

The boat come crashing back and I grabbed hold of one of the tires [attached to the float, Waszak said] *and shoved it up so it would force me into the water. When that thing come crashing back against the dock it tipped my hat—the old police hats we used to wear?—and it went over my eyes. That's how close it came . . . I just swam around the corner and climbed up.*

Waszak was lucky; George Buell, who had the job of boat lineman in the mid-50s, said he broke a hip when he fell into the water and the boat crashed into him. About 22 years later part of his hip was surgically replaced.

A pulley-operated gangplank attached to the dock at Fort Mason and angled down to the float. Because the tide changed so radically the walkway needed to move up and down, sometimes as much as nine feet. Often it hung in midair until someone walked on it or pulled it down to the floating platform where the boat moored.

"If you had bags and the tide was low!" Alma Ridlon declared, laughing. Alma was a German who immigrated to the United States after the war and lived on Alcatraz with her husband John, who manned the power house from 1960 until '63. They had two children, ages two and five:

I would tell my kids to stay in the car. I would unload my bags. Told them to stay in the car. Then I went down that gangplank which was about four feet off the platform, so it stood way up high and you grabbed it, and your weight and the groceries got it right down. You dropped your bag right quick and ran back before it would go up again [she laughed]. *You do that a couple of times. . .Then of course you waited for the boat.*

"On two or three memorable occasions there was no float and no plank to walk," recalled Phyllis McPherson Weed, whose step-father, Mac McPherson worked on

Alcatraz from 1942 until 1960:

Then the launch tied up tight against the pilings of the pier, and we climbed the ladder slats nailed to the pilings. Because such ladders were rarely used they were in poor repair. Some slats were loose, some missing altogether. And the damp, slime, tar and oil were hard on high heels, nylon hose, good clothes and clean hands. The last scramble over the raised edge of the pier totally destroyed any remaining shred of dignity.

In fact, dignity figured into a lot of encounters islanders had with the bay. Maryanne Waszak thought for a moment, then asked, "Whose color television went into the water?"

"That was 1959," Mahoney remembered later, chuckling. The *Warden Madigan*

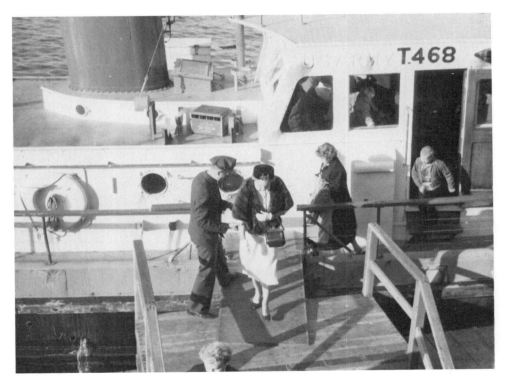

Alcatraz residents disembark from the island boat. (PHIL DOLLISON)

was not in service yet. Instead, the old *Warden Johnston,* a low-slung, beamy, class-T boat built especially for Alcatraz and used for most of the years it was a federal penitentiary, was in operation. A custodial officer had just purchased an $800-900 color console with a $90 service guarantee. Mahoney called it "the first color television set on Alcatraz." The man and his son were carrying it down the gangplank when the float moved out from under them and the set plunged into the drink, the kid with it. "Well, the float came back and it would have crushed the kid," Mahoney said, "but instead the TV set got crushed." Mahoney didn't know how they got the set out of the water or how damaged it really was; he arrived on the Fort Mason dock minutes later, seeing a shivering kid and a chagrined father. A year later, when the officer was transferred, Mahoney bought the set for $250-350, he said, and used it for the next

10 years.

Dozens of stories circulated about people accidentally dropping items in the water while getting on or off the boat. One man, carrying a brand new bunk bed mattress—still wrapped in paper—dropped it in the bay. "Yeah, and the tide was going out!" he said, remembering his panic. He retrieved it with a gaff. Another story circulated about a man whose wife slipped and fell in, ladened with a case of beer. Alcoholic beverages were against the employee rules on Alcatraz, but the man didn't hesitate. When his wife bobbed up to the surface, he yelled, "Give me the beer! The beer!"

But most trips were uneventful. The little 90-person boat slowly thumped and jumped through the white caps, avoiding the freighters and sailboats, and returned to Alcatraz. Rounding the east side of the island, one could see the large "WARNING, U.S. PENITENTIARY" sign which forbade entrance by other boats. Nearby, always just outside the 200-yard marking buoys, were the bay cruisers filled with tourists. They rounded the island constantly while hundreds of people, binoculars in hand, crowded to one side, attempting to see what they could on Alcatraz. It always seemed as if those boats listed a little.

"You'd hear this speaker," said LuAnne Freeman, who was standing on the balcony of #64 with Betty Miller one day, waiting for the school boat to return. "We didn't hear the whole spiel because of the way the wind was blowing, except that 'those women on the island were really families of the inmates.' And Betty was ready to walk on water to clarify that!"

Life on Alcatraz was not so restrictive in the late 1950s and early 1960s when the boat ran as often as a bus. Earlier only 11 round trips went a day, and earlier still only seven or eight, and that demanded a thousand little changes in one's daily habits.

Island living was not conducive to making large household purchases either. When the boat circled the island people assembled their babies, their books and groceries, sometimes their Christmas trees or their new lamps, and readied to disembark from a slippery boat to another tar-papered gangplank up to the dock. If fog covered the island the four or five dock inmates who unloaded the island barges were absent. If not, they lined up just beyond us, waiting for us to pass, watching silently.

The boat waited for no one; that was the rub. The last scheduled trip of the night was the midnight run; later a 2:00 a.m. boat existed if a request came in soon enough. But teenagers especially were loathe to call the Control Center from the mainland (few families had telepone connections to the city) to request the 2:00 a.m., because

"They used to say that a haircut cost 'em $5," said Marvin Orr. "In those days they were 50 cents. But when they got through with the cut they had to wait for the boat, and they'd go to a bar, and by the time they'd catch the boat, it'd cost 'em five bucks."

it usually meant they had missed the midnight boat, and they'd have to ask the man in Control to call their parents as well. And the 2:00 a.m. option had only been a recent innovation. "You had to be back by the last boat or you stayed over," my brother Phil Dollison said once with a slight catch in his voice, remembering back to when he was a teenager on the island and no other boat left after midnight. "And sometimes that worked to your benefit and sometimes that worked to your detriment."

Many island kids remembered a few days when the seas were so rough the warden decided to give everyone a school holiday. Parents called the schools from payphones on the island and the kids gladly stayed home. Dolby remembered one such day; he and a friend sneaked on the boat and rode it back and forth all morning.

"They had some pretty rough rides," remembered Fred Mahan, "and sometimes our boat would get lost in the fog and we would have to ring the bell on the dock and the officers would have to go down on the shoreline and guide [it] in."

The mouth of the Golden Gate is one of the largest breaks in the California coastal mountains and provides a lane for storms and fog to pass into the bay. Indeed, much of the heaviest fog, occurring in summer, is sucked in by weather patterns about 80 miles northeast of San Francisco. The Sacramento valley heats up and when the hot air rises it attracts cooler air from the ocean through the Golden Gate.

"When the fog came in," Dolby said, "it wasn't just a little mist:

It was solid—roll right in. That coming right in under the Gate, and ships disappearing right into that fog bank. [One time] we started towards the island. Well, the fog around the island was overwhelming. Literally you couldn't see 20 feet. It was thick! We couldn't see the island. We went around several times, all the kids had life preservers on, people all over the island, yelling, 'This isn't it, you're at the beach, go back the other way.' We could hear 'em yelling. It took us about an hour-and-a-half.

"Oh my God!" exclaimed Alma Ridlon, "we got there in August and the fog started rolling in, and the blinds rattled and the bed vibrated! I could *not* sleep! [They lived about a hundred feet from a foghorn.] I used to count it. It was 30 seconds after mine blew that the other one blew on the other end. . . After six months I got used to the foghorn."

Dick and Maryanne Waszak had been living in Omaha, Nebraska, when he applied for the job and took the civil service exam:

Bill Long came to get us and he said, 'I want you to see what it looks like. People live there,' [Maryanne began]. I wasn't going to go. That was the most frightening experience of my life. Just the thought of walking onto that island.

They moved onto the island in November 1959. "We had no choice," she explained. "There was no survival in San Francisco." Dick was a junior officer and had a civil service rating of GS-6; he was making $4480 a year (or $2.15 an hour). "The day we moved on he worked the four-to-midnight shift:

We got to the island, our furniture was on the dock, we got one bed up and he took off [she continued]. I did not know how to light the gas stove. I had to feed the kids. . . It was like I was a stranger from a foreign land. And when he got home at midnight, we went down on the dock and he and I carried the furniture up.

They moved into #64 building, which by then was a dismal apartment building. Twenty-seven apartments made up the three-story stone edifice that rose from the wharf. Because it had been coverted from a barracks it had many blind halls, dead-end stairways, and blocked-up fireplaces.

My family moved into #64 in 1954, as did all new residents. Each waited until one of the nicer apartment in the newer buildings A, B, or C, or the cottages, opened up. My family left the island after a year-and-a-half, however, and moved to the mainland, where other employees lived. (We returned in 1961 when my father became the associate warden, and lived in the more gracious, Spanish-style duplex at the east end of the island.) Although some of the corner apartments were large and well-positioned for an exquisite view, few people liked #64. The apartments had the kind of dinginess that wasn't easily covered by a coat of new paint.

Dick and Maryanne carried their furniture up the seven flights of stairs to their apartment on the first balcony.

"I weighed 98 pounds," Maryanne said. "We had an Amana freezer that he and I carried up together."

"We had a washer and a dryer," he remembered.

Waszak eventually worked in federal prisons in Florida, Kansas, and Tennessee before he retired in 1980. Maryanne was by then working in real estate, and their children were grown. Dick's red hair had turned a little lighter by then, but he still had his sunny disposition. "I fell apart after I retired," he kidded later. Like many prison officers who are under a lot of stress, he suffered several heart attacks and waited out a long recovery. He continued, remembering the day they moved on:

We moved into an apartment [in #64] and then we moved up to what they called the 'Cow Palace,' an 11-room apartment on the third floor of the building. It was a biggie.

"People on the island were getting a big break," said Officer Bob Fawson, who lived with his wife and family near the Waszaks at that time. "You got your apartment

Evelyn Dollison stands in 1962 at the associate warden's residence on one of the few patches of grass on Alcatraz, with the warden's residence and lighthouse in the background. (JOLENE BABYAK)

furnished with the utilities paid for $25 a month. There's no way you could beat that. Not in San Francisco."

If you took marbles or a ball [Maryanne continued] and you rolled them from the opposite end of the apartment, they would all roll towards the middle. [We paid] $21 a month.

"Everything was paid," Dick said, "plus we got our laundry done free."

They had an old torn-up apartment right there at the corner [Fawson continued]. That was your break-in. A lot of people had to live in that until something else came open. It was nearly always open because everyone was so anxious to get out of it. It was a real rat-hole. My wife cried when I showed it to her the first time. Then a fellow resigned and we had a real nice apartment.

Electricity was the biggest inconvenience on the island. Although Alcatraz generated its own power, the old diesel engine pumped out direct current. It could be counted on to blow toasters, irons, vacuum cleaners, TVs or stereos, often the moment they were plugged in. So alternating converters were purchased in the city. "Converters were a premium," Dick remembered:

And it appeared to me that while the Chief of Mechanical Service was telling everybody that you can't have converters because it draws too much on the DC system, it was kind of prestigious to have a nice big converter. And if you were in that inner circle you could have your big converter. Well, Al Severson was getting transferred and Al had a big converter for his organ. And I thought, by golly, if he can have a converter for his organ, I can have a

The dark alley moat at the fort level below #64 building, known from the Army prison-era as "Chinatown." Rumor had it that Army prisoners in the early 1860s were confined in cells here.

(PHOTO BY PHIL DOLLISON)

converter to wash diapers. Okay, we had a washer and a dryer but we obviously couldn't use them. Maryanne used the Amana freezer as a linen closet because we couldn't use that. We found a Maytag wringer washer with a DC motor on it and we used that until finally it died. So I packed it on my back one day, marched it out of #64 building, down the stairs to the dock and just deposited it right in the water. The tower man thought I'd gone bananas.

Waszak bought the converter and he and Pat Mahoney installed it after midnight one night so the CMS wouldn't catch them.

We put the washer and dryer in one of the bathrooms because it was a huge monstrous thing [Dick said]. And the converter was too big to be lugging it from room to room, and if we wanted waffles, we went into the bathroom and made our waffles.

I used to mash my potatoes in there [said Maryanne].

Fred "Fritz" Freeman was 25 years old when he and LuAnne, 24, moved on the island in 1959. They had four children.

It was spooky because we came over after hours one day to look at the apartment, and you know how #64 building looked, [said LuAnne]. It didn't look like your Nob Hill apartments, but under the circumstances we were made to believe we were very, very fortunate to get it because there were so many on the waiting list.

Fred Freeman had been in the Yuba City, California sheriff's department when he took the civil service exam for the appointment at Alcatraz. It was his first prison assignment. The year they moved on the island, Fred said, he just skirted being knifed in a cell house incident and it scared him enough to quit the service. He was out 14 months but kept thinking that if others

Residents almost always needed keys to gates around their compound. The alley moat is two stories below the railing at right.
(CORINNE EDWARDS)

could tough it out, so could he. He returned and remained with the federal prison service until he retired in January 1983. We talked the summer before he retired in their home on the reservation of the U. S. Penitentiary at Terre Haute, Indiana. It was their sixth prison:

I had a different attitude when we came back [LuAnne said]. I think both of us had learned a lot. As far as being afraid, I kept my doors locked, and I don't here. I didn't at Leavenworth and we had trash men come. I didn't at Texarkana, and heavens, we had yard men there. I think [it has] to do with maturing a little. But I didn't worry about the children on the island because we knew the only inmates out were on the dock.

One time I was scared. I came out on the balcony [of #64] and went up on the second balcony to go to Betty Howell's for a permanent. Fred was the dock officer that day, and as I walked out an inmate nudged Fred and Fred looked at me. I remember him doing it. And when he came home that night, I said, 'How did that inmate know?' And he said, 'Honey, they know more about us than you'd believe.'

All islanders had similar stories.My father thought it was uncanny that prisoners could learn so much so fast. Whenever FBI men landed on the dock—in those days of J. Edgar Hoover they were easy for us to recognize in their impeccably well-tailored dark suits—prisoners all over the island would know it before the agent got to the prison, he said. Mary McCreary Duggal, who was a teenager on the island when I lived there, said that a popular song one year contained the lyrics "All night, all day MaryAnne. . . " and she was embarrassed once to hear a prisoner on garbage detail near her apartment whistling the tune.

All the women on the island—and I knew most of them [said LuAnne Freeman]—it was none of this smiling at them or anything else. The inmates didn't even attempt to speak to you—they just didn't.

Unlike other prisons and farms where many unattended trustees are out all day, no Alcatraz prisoner was ever left unattended. Occasionally an island pick-up truck passed by with a guard at the wheels and two inmates on the sideboards, but even then a fence stood between them and us. We were not permittted to talk to each

Children from Alcatraz ride on their way to schools in San Francisco. An island school was considered from time to time but never implemented.
(PRINTED IN COLLIER'S MAGAZINE, AUG.1954; WILLIAM R. WOODFIELD, PHOTOGRAPHER)

other. We didn't have to be told. My childhood feelings of awe and hushed reverence became more complicated as I grew older and returned to the island. I felt embarrassed for them and tried not to look at them .

Nonetheless, all prisoners start to look the same after a while. You don't look long enough, especially if you are a teenage girl, to notice facial features, the cut of the chin, who looked like a con, who was handsome. Prisoners dressed the same, had the same caps, the same Navy pea coats, the same, it seemed, searching eyes.

A modicum of contact did occur, however. I remember one dock inmate who used to bow low and tip his hat when he saw one of us kids on the balcony of #64. Some boys had more contact than the rest of us. And sometimes that was not without repercussions, however, as Dolby showed in another account:

Kids weren't supposed to have toy guns over there, and I had a sort of a silhouette of a toy gun. I forget if we made it, but it didn't really qualify as a toy gun in my point of view. I dropped it over the balcony onto the dock, so I called down to one of the cons—said, 'Say, can you get that for me?' And I took a fishing line and lowered it down to the dock and had him hook it on and about the time he was hooking my gun onto the fishing line [Associate Warden] Miller walks along. He sees this con fumbling with a gun and he got a little excited over that!

I think that particularly realistic-looking silhouette I was told to get rid of, it didn't really qualify as a non-toy gun.

Seemingly ordinary concerns took on exaggerated meaning on an island prison. Garbage could not be discarded simply. Inmates were restricted to few reading materials, so residents' newspaper and magazines had to be bundled and put out with the laundry on Saturday morning rather than thrown in the garbage. Neither could cutlery, razor blades, saw blades or other tools, bottles, glassware or clothing be randomly thrown

Prisoners and residents rarely had contact, although sometimes when an inmate detail worked on the parade ground they could see each other. (PHOTOGRAPHER UNKNOWN)

away. Razor blades, because they were concealable yet particularly damaging, were thrown in the bay or disposed of off the island.

Firearms, of course, were the greatest hazard. Personal firearms were kept in the Control Center, and officers had to be reminded from time to time not to carry pocket knives. Toy guns and water pistols were strictly forbidden.

LuAnne Freeman recalled an incident that occurred right after they moved on the island. Their neighbors, the Millers, had a little boy named Skip. (Harold Miller, his wife Betty and their children lived on the island in the last years while he was a junior officer. Nearly 20 years later he was warden at the U.S. Penitentiary at Marion, Illinois.) "My daughter, Patty, was a brand new little neighbor so Skip promptly went in and under his bed pulls out this wooden toy pistol that he had no business having:

Of course Harold allowed him to have it under penalty of death if he took it out the door. Well, as kids will do, he went barreling out of his house with that pistol and Patty was right behind him. And of all places for him to go, he went right on the lower tier of #64 building, down by the post office. And who should be standing there, as usual, but the 'balcony lieutenant.' She took the gun and the kids came back crying. . .Well, Fred figured he was fired for sure.

[That woman] was totally efficient and she did end up being a lieutenant. She went into the prison service after her husband passed away. She started at Terminal Island and the last we heard of her she was a lieutenant at Alderson. But she was as good as gold. She gave free ice cream every Saturday morning during the summer, and we never knew for the longest time who was paying for it. The kids all got free ice cream. But I was totally afraid of that woman. . .She knew who went on the bus, who went on the boat, and who came home.

She always wore a fur coat with thongs, and her hair was cut with no curl to it. She usually had a cigarette and a cigarette holder. I don't mind telling you I could draw a picture of her, because I was young and had those four kids and I wasn't physically afraid of her, I just wanted to give her as wide a berth as possible because she didn't radiate friendship to me. She was real different. But I understand

Fences were a part of everyone's lives. (CORINNE EDWARDS)

Left: Electrician Frank Brunner walks from the warden's residence towards the prison building. The warden's residence, built in 1929 when Alcatraz was a military post, was of lovely California Mission-style architecture. Note the snow tracks on the concrete and roof; it seldom snows in the San Francisco Bay Area. (COURTESY OF PHIL DOLLISON)

Right: Although Alcatraz was mostly rock and concrete, the trees and shrubs planted during the military post days flourished in the moist, fresh air.

(PHOTO BY JOLENE BABYAK)

she made a fantastic officer, which doesn't surprise me. . . . She took that gun away from those kids and I proceeded after her and I said, 'It's not yours!' And she said, 'It's going up top!' and Betty [Miller] kept yelling that we were gonna' get fired . . . And she called up top and they sent George Black after it. Well, the gun never made it up top.

LuAnne learned other lessons through her children. Prisoners' visitors didn't show up very often. Many men had lost contact with their families. A surprising number were from the Midwest and East and families couldn't or wouldn't travel to Alcatraz for an hour-and-a-half visit a month. When they did arrive, on the boat or on the squat blue bus that made a round of the island after the boat docked, they were easily recognizable. Those whom I saw were often well-dressed, distant and perfunctory. They may have been afraid of us, the guards' children, or a little embarrassed. Then too, they may have in fact been coping with a boatful of children. Nonetheless, there was little contact between us and them, though many of us were curious about them:

Patty and June and I were riding up on the bus [LuAnne began], and this sharp-looking girl—she was in her early 20s and very, very pretty. I didn't see the diamond on her finger, but having a young daughter, she did. So the girls whispered to me, 'Who's that?' And I, from past exposure, said that it was Mickey Cohen's girlfriend. The kids were all in school and they were old enough to know who he was because that was prison talk around the house. So June meanders up the aisle of the bus before I could get her, and she said to this girl with the diamond ring, 'Did Mickey buy that for you?'

I was just destroyed!

The common gaffes, the restrictions, the little notoriety, all reinforced the bonds that brought people together. It could be patently restrictive at times, and more than one woman complained of the enforced confinement. Women and children were forbidden on the shoreline during daylight hours while prisoners were out of their cells. Families were not permitted dogs or cats.

It was a limited existence for children. Officially they were not permitted to play in the building hallways, despite the often dismal weather, never permitted to play on the dock, beyond the fence, up near the prison, or down by the sea. That relegated them to the parade ground. "Touch football," said Dolby. "That was really exciting on concrete." Little kids had bicycles; few of the older kids had them, there was no place to go. Of course there were no cars. Now and then a kid got to go up to the lighthouse and crank up the light. Sometimes the most vivid memories of island living were the smallest ones. All the kids remember collecting bumble bees and snails in jars, and pouring salt on the fat, doleful slugs that resided on The Rock. "Oh God! The slugs!" exclaimed one women who lived there during the 1950s. "That's about all I remember about Alcatraz."

The camaraderie shared by officers was also felt by islanders, however, and sometimes that spilled out onto the parade ground. The kids were used to seeing their dads walk down from prison in their dark uniforms. Although some men had difficulty losing the officiousness that permeated their working day, others never lost their insouciance, especially around kids. I can remember one dad coming down the hill in his dark uniform, ceremoniously taking off his prison jacket, hitting a baseball and running around the bases before begging off with a mock complaint about his

Island teenagers and friends pose at Christmas, 1949.
(COURTESY OF PAT BERGEN ROTHSCHILD)

advanced age. Phyllis Hess, who lived on Alcatraz from 1934 until 1938 remembered the day her dad, George Hess, M.D., the Chief Medical Officer, and Capt. Henry Weinhold decided she should learn to fly a kite. "They became so engrossed in flying it themselves that they forgot I was there," she said. "I just sat down, amused, and watched two usually dignified men romping around, yelling, 'Heh, look what I made it do!'" At Christmas time, dads could be seen helping the younger children learn to ride their bikes, or giving us pointers on fly casting.

But mostly kids looked for ways to entertain themselves.

"We used to walk on the balcony [railing]," said Dolby, when asked what he did for fun. "You know—tightrope walk. One side was about three feet down and the other side was two stories down. The man in the tower, god, I guess he was afraid to yell."

Popsicle sticks served as toy guns [he continued]. Instead of playing cops and robbers, we played prison. And we'd set up an area, play prison and have big break-outs. Eight or ten of us. You know, the 'guards' had guns and what the guards used for guns and what you tried to conceal when you got in so you could make your break and stuff, was a popsicle stick.

. . . Before I had my key [to the gates which let him up top to deliver newspapers], I discovered—now here's the world's total high security prison—I discovered you could unlock those locks with a popsicle stick. You shoved a stick in there, twisted it and it opened the lock. I called Miller or Madigan and said, 'I think there's something you might be interested in. . . ' [He laughs.] I gave 'em a demonstration and about two days later all the locks were changed.

"We worried about the kids, sure" said Jean Long, wife of Bill Long, and the island postmistress for many years. "Billy'd be down at the beach and back before you'd know it," she said of her ten-year-old.

Mike Pitzer in many ways typified a teenager on the island who looked for ways to entertain himself:

A lot of times we would go down [to the beach] and wave the sailboats to come past the markers. In fact, one time one came in and the guards kept yelling at the guy and he kept sailing in, and there was a whole bunch of people on his boat and they were drinking and stuff and waving and we were yelling at them. 'Cause that was one of our big jokes, to try to get the boats to come [past the marker]. Usually the [tower guard] would just get on the horn and warn them, but this group kept coming in and coming in. We started yelling, 'Go Back! Go back!' after we saw they were going to come all the way in, you know. Then the guard fired a couple of warning shots. One of them hit the main sail and just ripped it right down the center. Then they turned around.

Pitzer also talked about climbing with a friend around the rocks towards the Golden Gate side of the island, an area strictly off-limits particularly because a tower guard might mistake two teenagers for escapees. They were hauled into the warden's office and "chewed out," Pitzer said. "The lieutenant who was on duty said that if the [tower man] had been a younger guard, he would have probably opened fire on us." Pitzer explained that the incident occurred during the summer after the infamous 1962 Morris-Anglin escape.

There were rewards to living on Alcatraz, and the water figured into much of that. It was difficult to swim around the island, because of the numbing cold water, and also because there are no beaches on Alcatraz and the tides could be swift. But there was fishing, and plenty of it. "The Big Catch" is the title of one photograph taken on Alcatraz in 1957. Six men posed on the parade ground and among them are more than 25 striped bass.

"Oh, they used to catch those bass there," Marvin Orr said, remembering the particularly famous incident. "I was on duty on night:

*I was acting lieutenant and coming down the sea wall on the west side of the island about 2:00 in the morning. I threw my flashlight down in the water and you could see 'em. That water was **just wiggling** with bass. And I called Fred Mahan—he was quite a fisherman—and Fred called some other guys that like to fish and they came down and fished till daylight and they caught enough bass that night—the next morning they brought a pick- up truck down there and filled it full. And fed the main line [of the prison population].*

"Jeez, we just went hog wild," said Mike Pitzer. "I never caught so many fish in my life. There were quite a few of us down there 'cause I remember when they brought the dump truck down to haul all those fish up there."

"The sardines would come in," said Orr, "and the bass would follow 'em in, see:

And those runs'd only last about three hours, and when the sardines're gone, the bass're gone. And when daylight broke, these guys all along the bank, fishing you know, just—boy! you'd cast and you couldn't miss. You'd just pull them in just as fast as you could cast.

And these fishing boats outside the buoys [the San Francisco fishermen fleet]. There's no bass out there! And those guys're just going crazy out there! They're trying to edge in. The officer in the tower motioning— chasing them back, you know. They were just having a fit out there!

"I mean it was as fast as you could put your line out," said Long. "You could *not* get your line back without a fish on it:

It was the best one hour of fishing I had in my life. We actually had a pickup truck and we wheeled the fish out on a wheelbarrow up to where we could get a truck and took them to the dock and gave everybody all the fish they wanted there, and took the rest of them up and we fed the inmates all the fish they could eat.

And so it went. For much of the 29 years Alcatraz was a federal prison, life for us "involuntary inmates" was surprisingly placid. Our island life was similar to other neighborhoods in most ways. The city was close by and convenient. We commuted by boat, of course, instead of bus, but that was the major difference. And perhaps because of the sheer fortitude of the "balcony lieutenant," none of us ever fell into the bay.

Alcatraz residents, of course, talked about crime and criminals the way other people talked about the weather. Maybe it helped ease anxieties, and keep the danger at bay. But the 1950s and 60s, unlike the decades before or after, were not times of hostage-taking, after all. It may have occurred to some prisoners, Carnes once said, but it was an idea quickly rejected. No prisoner thought he'd get off the island alive.

And although Alcatraz had such an irreparably bad reputation, the kids took pride in their fathers' work—and for good reason. When my brother Phil Dollison was a teenager and living on the island, about 30 teenagers were in residence and about 10 of them went into law enforcement as a career. Several started out working at San Quentin State Prison, then moved into police work. Phil worked at San Quentin while he organized his own burglar alarm business in San Francisco. "I had one guy in San Quentin—an inmate who'd been at Alcatraz—tell me he'd much rather be in Alcatraz than San Quentin," Phil said. "He told me at least there he knew where he stood."

Our lives were not unlike those in the military service. Perhaps because our fathers felt that few outsiders understood their problems, prison people often remained insulated. Vacations in our household tended to include tours to other prisons where battle stories were relived—a hopelessly tedious practice in my mind then. And although our fathers only walked a few hundred yards to work in one of the most notorious cell houses in the nation, we gave little thought to the purpose of The Rock as anything other than our home. Except sometimes:

Bill Long, third from left, and five happy friends show off about 30 striped bass they caught off Alcatraz in the 1950s.
(PHOTOGRAPHER UNKNOWN; COURTESY OF JOHN BRUNNER)

I was working as captain's clerk [said Dick Waszak]. After the four o'clock count we were to feed the inmates and it was precarious because all the inmates would be in the dining room at that time and if any problems were to start, not only was staff down, but you'd have all the inmates out. And Blackwell was warden and he was also working late this one night and the three-deuce alarm went off . . . That's the standard alarm . . . And of course any time the alarm goes off, your adrenaline starts pumping.

. . . So I jumped over a railing, got to the phone and answered it and I could hear what sounded like kids in the background. Obviously it was somebody playing with the phone. So I fussed at them for a moment and told them to get off the phone. And seconds later it rang a second time. And of course my reaction was the same. You're really not sure whether someone's play- ing games or whether we actually have a problem. And I could still hear these kids. I made the comment to the warden that, by gosh, if they were my children, I'd sure take care of things. About that time the three-deuces goes off again, and I said, **'You kids get off this telephone!'** *I says,* **'Now who is this?'** *And a little guy on the other end says, 'This is Mike, Daddy, will you come play with me?' And it was my own son!*

No we didn't really *worry* about escapes—except sometimes.
"When they had a call for an emergency up top," said Bill Long, "everybody went just the way they were:

When we had a disturbance, [if] we were at a party, we didn't put on coats or anything, we just went right up the hill. They used to call down at #64 building and the phone was right outside my apartment and we answered the phone and they'd say, 'We have trouble in the cell house,' and that's all they had to say. Everybody available went. . .They'd hit the deuces and the deuces would go off and the Control Center man would make a decision what to do. . .

Four Alcatraz children, identified as Bob Orr, Don Martin, Don Fouler and O.P. Flynt, play atop one of the Rodman guns left over from the military post days.

(NATIONAL MARITIME MUSEUM)

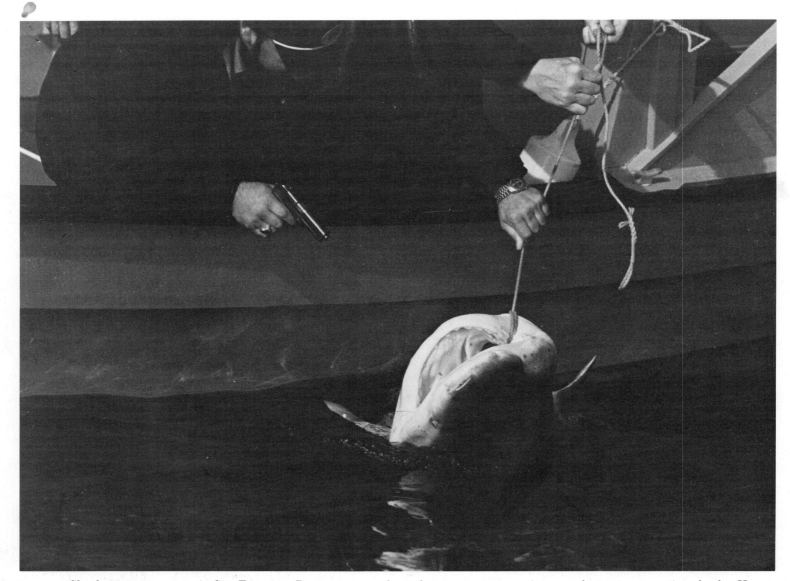

Sharks are as common in San Francisco Bay as rumors about them were among prisoners—but not man-eating sharks. Here a fisherman shoots a sand shark. (JOLENE BABYAK)

5

Escape Attempts 1934-1946

December 1937

"You know what kind of characters you had up there," George Steere said, "but when that old sir-reen takes off, you didn't know what was going on. " Steere, 12 years old at the time, had lived on the island about a year when the first escape siren sounded. (This was actually the second attempt for the federal prison, but the first in which convicts left the prison compound and made it as far as the bay. Joe Bowers allegedly attempted to climb a fence to freedom when he was shot by a tower guard on April 27, 1936. He fell to his death.)

Steere's home was the old Army hospital up by the prison which was torn down in the early 1940s. "Our dining room used to be the operating room," he said many years later. "We were right outside the prison, by the morgue."

The siren sounded on December 16, 1937. Theodore Cole, #AZ 258, a small 23-year-old man convicted of kidnapping and transferred from Leavenworth on the same shipment as Ralph Roe, #AZ 260, a 29-year-old man convicted of bank robbery reportedly doing 99 years, broke out of an industrial shop, dropped down to the bay, and vanished.

"Blackie" Audett claimed to have been watching from the other end of the shop when he saw them jump from the window. He wrote in his book that he saw Ralph Roe hit the water and come up about 25 yards later, already floundering, and then watched him disappear into a fogbank just as the prison siren screamed out the escape.

Steere knew instinctively what to do. He didn't go outside. He sat, waiting, with a baseball bat in his hand.

Joyce Rose Ritz was on a city bus returning to Alcatraz from junior high school in

San Francisco when she saw an early newspaper headline. By that time, down at the bottom on Van Ness Avenue where the boat docked in those early days, a guard was waiting for all kids to assemble. "They were always afraid of the kids being kidnapped so they kept a pretty good watch on us." Ritz said. "The little ones used to go to schoool in a cab."

After what seemed like an interminably long boat ride, she and other children whose mothers were working in the city were herded into a house by a guard and told to stay put. All available men went immediately to the prison when the escape siren sounded. All others stayed inside and locked their doors. The island telephones were off limits. It was a tense time; residents were already somewhat confined and now they were prisoners in their own homes until the convicts were located, or presumed off the island.

"We were sitting, talking, and suddenly I looked up and saw the door open—we were all petrified—and two of us girls dove underneath the kitchen table, another ran into the bedroom. One of the older boys picked up a big piece of wood and [ran] to the door—ready to hit someone." Joyce Ritz would hear the Alcatraz siren sound a few more times before she moved off the island in 1951. But this was her first experience. She laughs about it now. The door slowly opened on the frightened children, and a friendly face appeared. It was an officer, making the mandatory search of each apartment.

Officers continued searching for about a week, but Roe and Cole were never heard from again. They were presumed drowned.

In its 29-year federal prison history, Alcatraz had 14 officially-cited escape attempts involving 36 men; seven were killed by gun shots, one drowned, 21 were returned, two were returned and executed, and five are still missing and presumed dead—Roe and Cole in 1937 and Frank Morris and the Anglin brothers in 1962. Throughout the years prisoners tried various ways to get off the island, until after a while the stories became a part of their collective knowledge of what worked and what didn't. It was only a matter of time, as the prison grew older, before they hit on the right combination.

May 1938

Five months later, on May 23, another escape attempt occurred. James C. Lucus, #AZ 224, serving 30 years for bank robbery and kidnapping, Thomas Limerick, #AZ 263, on a life sentence for bank robbery and kidnapping, and Rufus "Whitey"

Prisoners leaving the industries area, which was contained in two buildings—the "new" industries, left foreground, and the old model building in the background. Each day they walked through several metal detectors. (COURTESY OF PHIL DOLLISON)

Alcatraz was not a rehabilitative prison; industries was almost an afterthought. Shops here generally handled one or two contracts at a time, or in the case of the brush, and the glove shop, above, were satellites of the main factories in Leavenworth and Danbury. (PHIL DOLLISON)

Franklin, #AZ 335, doing 30 years for bank robbery, caught Officer Royal Cline in a disadvantaged moment. Lieutenant Isaac Faulk later speculated that Cline was talking to another prisoner, because he was hit in the back of the head with a claw hammer. "They sunk that right in his skull," Faulk said. The trio got nowhere for their troubles. Limerick was fatally shot in the head storming the Model Tower; Lucas and Franklin gave up and were eventually tried. Cline, however, was dead.

Now a veteran of two escape attempts on Alcatraz, Joyce Ritz found it all very exciting. A subtle change occurred among the children of the guards, however. Cline had kids. His death drove home the realization that it could happen to anyone's father.

January 1939

Federal prison officers only made $1680 a year in the 1930s, whether they worked a minimum security prison or a hardship post like Alcatraz. The fourth escape attempt in 33 months occurred on January 13, 1939. This time the escape siren sounded at about 2:30 a.m.

Five men, serving a combined 229 years, broke out of segregation cells, then broke out a cell block window. Arthur "Doc" Barker, #AZ 268, serving life for kidnapping, Dale Stamphill, #AZ 435, life for kidnappping, Henri Young, #AZ 244, 20 years for bank robbery, William Martin, #AZ 370, 20 years for post office robbery and Rufus McCain, #AZ 267, 99 years for kidnapping and bank robbery, scrambled down the island cliffs to get to the bay.

For a moment the escape siren mingled with the foghorn and caused some confusion. Suddenly everyone was awake. Esther Faulk got up with her husband. George Steere got up. The Roses were up. Later Joyce Ritz and her mother walked outside for a peek at the boats circling the island and got locked out.

Ernest Padgett was on patrol that night, armed with a .45 calibre Army automatic. It was foggy, he recalled in a written story later, and when the siren sounded he telephoned the Control Center and got word of the missing five men. Suddenly his automatic felt like a toy. Warden Johnston was up, of course, and he recalled later that the fog was as thick as a "mass of wool." Joyce Ritz and the Faulks remembered it being a clear night, at least on some parts of the island. Alec Klineschmidt, an elderly man when interviewed, insisted it had been foggy. "You could hear the tin cans rattle," he said, recalling his most vivid memory of the shooting down at the beach.

Prisoners there were trapped between guards shooting from the parade ground and from the island boat.

All five scattered when the firing began. Stamphill and Barker, Stamphill later said, were pinned behind some rocks. Barker peeked up and was shot in the forehead. Stamphill was eventually released from the federal system and lived in the Midwest. When interviewed he said that Barker turned around and warned him not to get up, then talked for what seemed like an hour before he lost consciousness.

While this occurred, Faulk and Deputy Warden Ed Miller moved down a trail that led to the shore. At one point they waded into the water and suddenly, behind them, Martin accidentally fell down the embankment. Startled, Faulk later chuckled about the "capture." Like the other prisoners, Martin had removed his clothing to make tie strips for the raft they were trying to build. The two officers escorted the naked, cold, and humiliated man through the parade ground up to the prison.

The still-conscious Barker, and Stamphill, wounded in the knees, were soon loaded onto a dinghy behind the island boat, and dragged to the dock on the other side of the island. This time, the guards had clearly won. (It was a dubious victory, however, and a low point in Alcatraz escape history. Officials hadn't retooled the soft cell bars in segregation as they had the other cell fronts when they took over the prison. Niether apparently was there a guard present at night—or he was sleeping— a disturbing oversight in the nation's most secure prison.)

Win or lose, however, the events in these years sealed the reputation of Alcatraz; it would never be an easy place to do time—for convict or guard. There might be light moments, as when Joyce Ritz and her mother were locked out of their apartment during the attempt and Ritz tried to climb in the window and suddenly, out of the dark, stepped an armed guard who shouted, "Hold it!"

"Here I am half in and half out and my mother was jumping up and down, shouting, 'Don't shoot! Don't shoot!'" The story became one of their private adventures during a time when the headlines shouted out the news that the notorious "Doc" Barker was dead on Alcatraz.

May 1941

Four convicts, all life-termers, bound and gagged a shop foreman and Captain Paul J. Madigan, and attempted to saw through industry window bars on May 21, 1941. Two of them Joseph Cretzer, #AZ 548, and Sam Shockley, #AZ 462, were desperate to get off Alcatraz; Cretzer would be killed and Shockley executed for a later escape attempt on The Rock.

Both attempts were weak and ended in failures. But it accelerated one career. The captain of the guards, Paul Madigan, had been hand-picked by Warden Johnston to work Alcatraz. He had attended college, and this little edge was enough to alert the Bureau of Prisons. But what caught everyone's eye was this escape attempt.

Madigan was a tough but genuinely warm Irishman with a freckled face. He was a thoughtful man who smoked a pipe. He lit it often, then forgot to puff, and had to light it again, thus giving himself ample time to think before speaking. When he got a little mad or agitated, he gritted his teeth, my father said later, "and broke a lot of pipe stems that way." According to his daughter, that same year he was promoted to associate warden and sent to the federal prison at Terminal Island. A year later he transferred to another federal institution at Sandstone, Minnesota. By promotion and transferring off Alcatraz in 1941, he missed two escape attempts in which he might have been injured or killed. In one, the disastrous 1946 shoot-out, Capt. Henry Weinhold was critically injured from a gunshot while being held prisoner with other officers.

Madigan transferred back to Alcatraz twice more, however, eventually as warden. He became known as "Promising Paul" to prisoners and officers alike. He was a religious man, a Catholic who went to church on the island often, but the moniker was more a tribute to his finesse as a politician. "You'd go to him with a problem," my father, who was then superintendent of industries, explained:

He'd listen, seem to approve of your solution and you'd go out satisfied. Later someone else would go in with the same problem, only on the opposite side. He'd leave satisfied and you'd find out you came out on the short end of the stick. After that happened

Fourth grade pay generated 10 cents an hour in 1953; first grade, the top grade, earned a man 25 cents in 1953 and 30 cents an hour in 1959. (Long term industrial time generated an extra five cents an hour.)

Despite the low wages, Ben Rayborn, a former prisoner and later a successful para-legal in San Diego, said he helped put his daughter through college on what he earned. (PHIL DOLLISON)

An officer and three culinary inmates help load food supplies into the cell house basement. (NATIONAL MARITIME MUSEUM; BETTY WALLER COLLECTION)

many times, I learned to be the last one to talk with [him], and my average improved quite a bit.

Luck continued to be with Madigan. He was warden at Alcatraz from 1955 until 1961, then was transferred, leaving his associate, Olin G. Blackwell, as warden during the last disastrous year on Alcatraz.

Tied up, but conscious, in this 1941 escape attempt Madigan coolly told the foursome that their cutting tools would not measure up to the bars, and repeatedly reminded them that they would soon be found to be "out of pocket," anyway. Frustrated, they gave up, never getting out of the industries building.

September 1941

Four months later, John Richard Bayless, #AZ 466, jumped off the dock. Like most convicts attempting to escape Alcatraz, he hadn't counted on the bay being so cold and choppy. "He got a couple of hundred feet," remembered Marvin Orr, "and turns around and swims back! And winds up in the hole. It was too cold for him, see!"

April 1943

Captain Weinhold was surprised, bound, and gagged on April 14, 1943. Four men, Harold M. Brest, #AZ 380, serving life for bank robbery and kidnapping, Floyd Hamilton, #AZ 523, 30 years for bank robbery, Fred Hunter, #AZ 402, serving 25 years for postal robbery and James Boarman, #AZ 571, serving 20 years for bank robbery, were down by the bay by the time Weinhold was able to get loose and blow his whistle.

A tower guard shot, and that day Warden Johnston was quoted announcing the drowning deaths of Boarman and Hamilton, and the recapture of the others.

But Hamilton was to have another fate.

Once linked with Bonnie and Clyde, Hamilton was a tall man with deep-set eyes. He was intelligent, soft-spoken, and later practiced yoga in his cell. He had not sunk into the water and died. Instead he swam back to the island, hid in a cave for two days where the high tides trapped him. He left his cave finally, climbed the hill back to the prison and fell asleep in the old model building. Weinhold, in a comic moment of supreme irony, discovered him sleeping next to the radiator.

August 1943

In the next attempt, Huron "Ted" Walters, #AZ 536, serving 30 years for bank robbery, was surrounded by officers just as he was ready to launch himself into the bay, said a prison report, with "a couple of cans tied to his waist for buoyancy." Although a lame attempt and not properly thought out, Walters had put some thought into the swim.

July 1945

John Giles, #AZ 250, a bright, pleasant 25-year-termer for post office robbery, whom officers generally liked for his "good attitude," had one of the better inmate jobs; he worked in the laundry as an inmate dockworker. Over many months he collected pieces of Army clothing from the laundry. By July 31, he had assembled the entire uniform, and quietly boarded the *Frank M. Coxe,* the U.S. Army boat that docked almost daily at Alcatraz in the earlier days. His absence was immediately noticed however, and Deputy Warden E.J. Miller sped over to Angel Island on another boat to meet Giles there. This remained the most ingenious attempt to escape from Alcatraz until the Morris-Anglin attempt in June 1962. Some officers even expressed a bit of guarded admiration for the man, but he was severely punished for his little boat ride. Giles lost 3000 days good time, according to a later prison report, which amounted to more than eight years, and he received an additional three years. When he got out of D block two years later, he worked one of the worst jobs—the incinerator.

May 1946

·The last escape attempt in the 1940s started in confusion and ended in tragedy. On May 2, 1946 Bernard Coy, #AZ 415, allegedly spread the bars into the gun gallery cage—where the only man inside the prison had a gun—knocked out Officer Bert Burch, and passed guns and keys down to his buddy. Joe Cretzer and Coy, one by one, surprised and overpowered other cell house officers and opened several cells. Prisoners Miran Thompson, Marvin Hubbard, Sam Shockley and Clarence Carnes joined Coy and Cretzer in the attempt.

The would-be escapists attempted to pick off the tower guards, missed, then panicked. Thompson and Shockley reportedly screamed at Cretzer to kill their witnesses, now about nine officers trapped inside two cells. Angered because they

One convict had a steel plate in his skull and regularly set off the metal detectors. Officers often let him pass through anyway, so other prisoners used him to pass contraband from industries to the cell house—so went one story. (COURTESY OF PHIL DOLLISON)

couldn't obtain the key to get out of the cell house, Cretzer steadied his gun and fired into the cells.

Capt. Weinhold was thrown against the cot as the bullet struck him in the chest; Lieutenant William Miller, who'd already been pistol whipped, was hit in the arm. Officer Corwin took a bullet in the face. Lieutenant Simpson was hit in the abdomen and officers Lageson and Baker were also shot. (Betty Weinhold Horvath wrote years later that her father, shot on her birthday, was hospitalized for months and retired with full disability. "He was never supposed to have lived through the injuries he sustained," she said. "The bullet entered his [chest], turning and passing through his right lung, thereby collapsing it, and then exiting under his armpit and re-entering his upper right arm, shattering the bone." Capt. Weinhold lived another 20 years before he died of a heart attack in 1967. He was involved in several escape attempts at Alcatraz, and injured in two of them. "My mother used to say that if there was an escape attempt going on, Daddy was sure to be involved.")

No one really knew what was going on, but within minutes there was no movement in the family compound. "We did know [prisoners] were shooting all over the place," remembered Marvin Orr, whose family was on the island at the time. "It wasn't safe to walk anyplace. They were shooting out the kitchen windows, out the cell house windows, out the hospital, shooting at the towers, at anything that moved," he said.

"As long as the place has been there," said Fred Mahan, an officer who spent 17 years on Alcatraz, "there [were] no families hurt. In the '46 riot, inmates got access to a phone, and called up some of the people, and told 'em they would be down. They were trying to get hostages, but they didn't get out [of the cell house] to do it."

The confusion showed in officials as well. Warden Johnston was not the leader of an assault team nor a trained battle strategist. He and Associate Warden E.J. Miller overcalculated on how many armed escapees were involved and loose inside the cell house. They sent an armed party to the side of the hill who were instructed to shoot into the cell house—a foolish decision because many uninvolved prisoners were trapped in their cells. They also sent a rescue squad into the cell house to release the trapped guards. Officers Bergen, Faulk, and Mahan were among others in the rescue team. But officers on the side of the hill were poorly managed, some did not hear the cease fire order when it came down, and quickly two officers were injured, one fatally. It was never determined who actually fired the weapon that killed Officer Harold B. Stites, who was a part of a rescue team, but some officers on duty at that time insisted that Stites was shot by a bullet from a guard on the hill.

The trapped officers in the two cells were eventually rescued, but William Miller, who originally had, and hid, the cell house key the prisoners needed to get out of the building, would later die of his wounds.

"Word came over that Mr. Miller had been killed," said Joyce Rose Ritz, who by then was an adult. She was home when the escape attempt began. The break trapped as many civilians on the island in their homes as islanders caught on the mainland. The regular scheduled island boat was interrupted, so few could come or go. Friends with Associate Warden E.J. Miller's wife, Joyce had crept over to their house, and they turned on the radio. "Word came over that Mr. Miller had been killed and we didn't know which one. I quickly grabbed the phone and called [up top] and said I was with Mrs. Miller and was it E.J? And they said 'No.' And I just hung up."

Reinforcements from San Quentin, Leavenworth, and McNeil Island were eventually summoned. Joseph Stilwell, Sixth Army commander, and Frank Merrill of the famed Merrill's Marauders offered advice, and Stilwell approved a request of 15-pound "shake" bombs. Ten cases of grenades and ten cases of carbine ammunition were reported by newspapers to have been rushed to Alcatraz from Benicia Arsenal. Influenced by the commandos who were using misplaced World War II tactics, Johnston approved the Marines, who by Friday were on the island to drop grenades from the roof into the cell house.

. . . They drilled this hole through the roof somewhere, or kicked out a window, or something [a prisoner later testified in San Francisco] *but they were throwing grenades down, and the grenades were hitting behind the cells, and they were hitting pretty close, because some gas had [come] in and I had advised the boy next door to me and the boy upstairs and my partner—the cell just below me—[that] the best way to get out of that gas was to clean the commode out and breathe the air from the commode. . . I did. I had mine cleaned out, all the water taken out, a towel laying over it, and I was sitting beside it.*

The bombing continued until no more shots were returned from the cell house. Saturday morning, May 4, officers found Coy, Cretzer and Hubbard dead in a utility corridor. Each had injuries and a bullet hole in his head. Coy was still dressed in an officer's uniform he had worn to fool guards. He was said to be still clutching his weapon.

Thompson, Shockley and Carnes were tried in December for the murder of William Miller. Thompson appeared surly. Lawyers based Shockley's defense on insanity

Bernard Coy, left, Joe Cretzer, center, and Marvin Hubbard, right, in mug shots and on guerneys after their deaths in 1946. (NATIONAL MARITIME MUSEUM)

Two who made it: former captain Phil Bergen, left, and former prisoner Clarence Carnes share a lighter moment on Alcatraz in the 1980s during the filming of Carnes' life story for television.

(JOLENE BABYAK)

and drummed up his mental incompetence but it was a weak defense. Neither man appeared sincere. They were executed at San Quentin for their part.

Carnes, #AZ 714, the 19-year-old Indian who had arrived at Alcatraz the year before with two life sentences, was the only prisoner to be spared—probably because of his youth. He was given his third life sentence, and at Alcatraz he was sent to segregation for seven years. He later said that officers who'd been involved in the mishap never mistreated him, but others, who'd not been involved, carried grudges.

He was transferred to Leavenworth when Alcatraz closed in 1963, was paroled in the late 1970s, misstepped, went back briefly, then was again released. We met one day in a fast food restaurant, despite my father's initial apprehension.

During the next eight years that I knew him he had a tumultuous life. He worked mostly in a Kansas City half-way house, was the subject of a television film about his life which generated appearances on national television shows which made him feel famous, was mugged, robbed, was on welfare, and suffered bouts of periodic alcoholism which aggravated his diabetes. One Saturday night in the midst of all this he called me, lonely and inebriated. "I'm sitting here, nothin' to do. And you know something? I had a better weekend, many a time, inside the penitentiary of Leavenworth than I'm having at this very moment. If I were in Leavenworth, I'd have some popcorn, or cookies, or a smuggled sandwich, and I'd be sitting at the TV with one of my friends, and be comfortable."

Carnes had spent all of his adult life in prison, and didn't really know how to cope with life on the outside where there were no guarantees.

In 1987, when his doctor said that because of his diabetes he probably wouldn't see two more birthdays, Clarence stole a little money and went on the lam, thus breaking parole. When he turned himself in, he was quickly sent to Springfield, Missouri, where there is a federal medical prison. There he received his much needed dialysis three times a week. His incarceration was a blessing of sorts.

None of the three would-be escapists were charged with the death of Officer Stites in 1946. The Bureau of Prisons promised an "exhaustive" investigation and did investigate, but the findings were never released. No one wanted to chastise publicly a prison administration nor its officers, among whom numbered at least 11 wounded and two dead, even if two men were suspected of accidentally being injured and killed by federal officers. It was not the Bureau's style to make exhaustive investigations and hold itself accountable. Not even if it meant aiding other prison officials, who would be involved in other riots that occurred across the country in the early 1950s.

Most accounts of the 1946 so-called "Battle of Alcatraz" have not dealt honestly with what really happened, perhaps because the older prison guards are suspicious of newspaper reporters. They were not reluctant to voice their opinions, however, to someone, like myself, who is considered "family".

Although Warden Johnston had had an almost exemplary prison career, this last major event showed that he was a shaky, 70-year-old man ill-equipped to handle such a crisis. He would soon retire. But more importantly, it showed that the Bureau of Prisons, despite its aura of professionalism, hadn't really prepared the staff of the nation's most secure prison for crisis management. This lack of preparation became a more acute problem as time slowly ground on.

Freedom was always just a fence and the treacherous bay away.
(COURTESY OF ART DOLLISON)

"No matter how many clothes you put on, you were always cold and damp," said Phil Bergen of the yard wall. Bergen said he was assigned to the yard wall for a "solid year" because someone told Ed Miller he was tough. "You couldn't get in the pill box very often . . . and there was no protection against the elements. My face was so raw I couldn't shave." (COURTESY OF PHIL DOLLISON)

6

The Morris-Anglin Attempt:
The Problem

For ten years after 1946, no escape siren sounded on the island. Then on **July 23, 1956**, Floyd P. Wilson, a lifer convicted of first degree murder, slipped away from the dock crew. He was found 12 hours later hiding in an island crevice along the beach. He wasn't able to put together a raft from the driftwood on the beach and the sash cord he had in hand.

Another attempt on **September 29, 1958** involved Aaron Burgett, #AZ 991, who arrived in August 1952 from Leavenworth as a Missouri postal robber, and Clyde M. Johnson, #AZ 864, a former "public enemy" from Indianapolis who transferred from Leavenworth in 1950. Johnson and Burgett were on a garbage detail with Officer Harold Miller. They surprised him, tied him up and allegedly debated killing him before they suited up for the swim. (Because the incident began near the parade ground and officers' quarters, it was potentially the most dangerous for families. But no hostages were taken; Burgett and Johnson were more interested in getting off the island immediately.)

Johnson wasn't the strongest swimmer [said Officer Fred Mahan]. *He didn't get that far and he just barely made it back. He edged himself along the beach and got in a little crevice there on the Golden Gate side and Christopherson and myself climbed about half way down that cliff, then worked ourselves horizontally around the island.*

There was a Coast Guard boat out there and they spotted him first. He was hiding in a crevice at the water's edge. They motioned to us and Chris and I climbed the rest of the way down the cliff and found him. That scared him so badly they had to send him to [the prison hospital] at Springfield.

"Johnson pretended to be in shock," said Clarence Carnes, "his mind had slipped:

He immediately went into this thing, even while they were putting him in the hole. But when the guard wasn't around, he was talking. Everybody knew what was going on including the guards, but what they knew and could prove was two different things.

. . . Johnson told everybody . . . Burgett had all this insulating stuff on and they each had a raincoat—with the idea that they could catch some air in a kind of turtle-back thing, and float. And Burgett put some plywood fins on his feet. He hit that water and the undertow got him. Took him down. He didn't come up.

What was left of Burgett was found two weeks later, floating face down in the water within yards of the island. Bill Long recollected, muttering sympathetically under his breath, "Burgett—ah—

He put winter underwear on, and covered that with axle grease he got out of the garage, and then put his clothes on, then his heavy 'brogan' shoes. He made swim fins from plyboard, and he wired those to the bottom of his feet. These things were on his feet when we picked him up!

He must have swam about 30 yards and gone down like a stone.

The body was identified by the numer imprinted on his tattered prison clothes. Inmate dockworkers saw the remains. My father told me later that a cloud of depression descended upon prisoners when they heard about it. It wasn't an emotional response to his death but a disappointment in the failure. Among the prisoners he was rumored to be one of the strongest, and he was healthy, so they figured he could make it.

Everyone talked about it. The officers weren't any happier about his death than the prisoners were sorry, but they were glad Burgett had failed. That was the intriguing part, my father said; his death was incidental to prisoners and employees alike. "It was his failure that counted."

By the late 1950s, when Burgett and Johnson made their attempt, the problem of getting federal prison officers to transfer to Alcatraz was becoming chronic. Sometimes employers would try anything to fill the gaps.

When Gregory transferred to Alcatraz in the mid-1940s, he arrived on a Saturday night and was put to work on Sunday. "I thought at least they'd give me Sunday off," he groused. "I didn't even know where the cell house was."

"We talked [about this]," Dick Waszak said, remembering when he applied to the prison service for a job. "We went over the list of prisons . . . and we said, 'Well, obviously they wouldn't send a guy who just fell off the truck to Alcatraz.' I mean, that's the biggie . . . And we put down 'anywhere in the United States.' . . .Never thinking that Alcatraz would be our assignment."

"We got the letter and handled it like a hot potato," said his wife.

"Scared the daylights out of us," he added.

Many men came to Alcatraz after passing a civil service exam. In some cases they could interview with the post office, the law enforcement or Alcatraz Penitentiary. "They called me over for an interview," said Bob Fawson. "I was amazed because I thought it would be awfully hard to get a job there. The captain interviewed me and I passed [the physical] easily, and when I came back down the first thing he said when I walked in his office was, 'You want to check out a uniform and go to work right away?'"

The problem was age-old. Turnover among prison guards was high. In a 1937-38 annual report at Alcatraz, Warden Johnson reported nearly an 18 percent turnover, and hinted that he didn't have enough men to establish a 48-hour work week. By the end of World War II, a Bureau of Prisons' annual report noted a 35 percent overall turnover among new recruits. The Bureau faced a genuine problem which it continued to address in reports to Congress, but about which nothing was done. (Despite such public laments, annual reports often contained as many as 30 tables of statistics on prisoners, yet statistics on prison officers were seldom collected or published.)

The gap widened in the 1950s when Art Dollison arrived. He transferred after putting "West Coast" on the application, feeling assured that since one of his colleagues had just gone to Alcatraz, he wouldn't. (Later

The Control Center was the nerve center, enclosed in bullet-proof sheet steel and plate glass. Nothing happened without the Control Center officer's knowledge. All prison counts, all keys, firearms, and ammunition were checked out here. Even the island boat officer checked with Control before departing. (PHIL DOLLISON)

UNITED STATES DEPARTMENT OF JUSTICE
BUREAU OF PRISONS

TEN DAY MENU

For the Period __March 21st__ To __March 31, inclusive__   A. M. DOLLISON Estimated Population __2 7 5__

ASSOCIATE WARDEN

NOTED
APR 1 6 1962

Day and Date	BREAKFAST PATTERN: (* Optional) Fruit or Juice; Cereal; Fresh Milk; Special Bread and/or Main Dish; Bread; Oleo; Jam*; Syrup*; Sugar; Beverage.	Amt. of Main Ingredient	DINNER PATTERN: (* Optional) Soup*; Juice*; Main Course; Sauce or Gravy*; Oleo*; Potato or Substitute; Vegetable; Salad*; Relish or Pickles*; Bread and/or Rolls; Dessert; Beverage.	Amt. of Main Ingredient	SUPPER PATTERN: (* Optional) Soup*; Juice*; Main Course; Sauce or Gravy*; Oleo*; Potatoes or Substitute; Vegetable; Salad; Bread and/or Rolls Dessert; Beverage.	Amt. of Main Ingredient
WED 21	Choice of Dried Fruit Choice of Dry Cereal Steamed Farina Fresh Milk French Toast Hot Syrup Toast – Butter Sugar Coffee		Split Pea Soup – Crackers Creamed Chicken Giblets Fried White Rice Seasoned Fresh Spinach Hot Biscuits – Butter Lettuce & Tomato Salad French Dressing Fruit Custard Milk Drink – Tea – Bread		Baked Swiss Steak Whipped Potatoes Brown Gravy Buttered June Peas Catsup – Mustard Cabbage & Pepper Salad Sweet Cream Dressing Vanilla Ice Cream Milk Drink – Coffee & Cream – Bread	
THU 22	Choice of Dried Fruit Choice of Dry Cereal Steamed Hominy Grits Fresh Milk Danish Roll Toast Butter Sugar Coffee – Bread		Yankee Bean Soup – Croutons Brown Beef Stew Buttered Egg Noodles Steamed Cauliflower Harvard Beets Catsup – Chili Pods Green Onions – Radishes Bread Pudding w/ Lemon Sauce Milk Drink – Tea – Bread		Boiled Fresh Corned Beef Parsley Buttered Potatoes Creamed Cabbage Buttered Carrots Catsup – Horseradish Tossed Green Salad – Russian Dressing Raisin Spice Cake Milk Drink – Coffee & Cream Whole Wheat Bread	
FRI 23	Choice of Dried Fruit Choice of Dry Cereal Rolled Oats Fresh Milk Hot Cakes Hot Syrup Toast – Butter Sugar Coffee – Bread		Beef Barley Soup – Croutons Chili Con Carne Sliced Cheddar Cheese Baked Macaroni Seasoned Rapini Greens Baked Banana Squash – Catsup – Mustard Cucumber & Onion Salad Cherry Jello w. Meringue Milk Drink – Tea – Bread		Grilled Fillet of Perch Tartar Sauce – Lemon Wedges Baked Idaho Potato Buttered Green Beans Corn Muffins – Butter Creamed Cole Slaw Catsup – Chili Pods Chocolate Cream Pie Milk Drink – Coffee & Cream – Bread	
SAT 24	Choice of Dried Fruit Choice of Dry Cereal Steamed Cornmeal Fresh Milk Raised Donuts Toast Butter Sugar Coffee – Bread		Fresh Vegetable Soup – Croutons Grilled Bacon & Tomato Sandwich Lyonnaise Potatoes Cream Style Corn Glazed Parsnips Mustard – Catsup Lettuce Wedges – Mayonnaise Cocoanut Custard Milk Drink – Tea – Bread		Barbequed Spare Ribs Fried Hominy Braised Sauerkraut Buttered Zucchini Hard Rolls – Butter Mustard – Catsup Green Onions – Radishes Fresh or Canned Fruit Milk Drink – Coffee & Cream – Bread	
SUN 25	Fresh Fruit Choice of Dry Cereal Rolled Oats Skim Milk Toast Butter Apricot Jam Sugar Coffee – Bread		Southern Fried Chicken – Sage Dressing Showflake Potatoes Giblet Gravy Buttered Asparagus Cloverleaf Rolls – Butter Cranberry Sauce Sliced Tomatoes Cottage Pudding w/ Fruit Sauce Coffee & Cream – Bread		Brown Bean Soup – Croutons Assorted Luncheon Meats Club Salad Hot Mixed Vegetables Celery Hearts – Carrot Curls Mustard – Catsup Strawberry Ice Cream Coffee & Cream – Bread	
MON 26	Choice of Dried Fruit Choice of Dry Cereal Steamed Hominy Grits Fresh Milk 2 Fried Eggs Hash Browned Potatoes Toast – Butter Sugar – Catsup		Chicken Rice Soup – Croutons Grilled Cheese Sandwich Baked Pork & Beans Seasoned Turnip Greens Stewed Okra & Tomatoes Chopped Romaine w/ 1000 Island Dressing – Mustard–Catsup Lemon Pudding w/ Meringue		Grilled Beef & Pork Sausage O'Brien Potatoes Brown Gravy Buttered Cabbage Glazed Carrots Catsup – Mustard Chilled Spiced Beets	

Holiday Activities

ALCATRAZ ISLAND

December . . . 1962

Preceding page: Part of a 1962 ten-day menu for 275 prisoners on Alcatraz.

This page: The Christmas Day menu printed in the Alcatraz print shop. The meal was the same year to year. (BOTH FROM ART DOLLISON)

Christmas Eve

Christmas packages will be distributed, courtesy of the Director, Prison Industries and the Warden.

Christmas Day

Recordings and selected radio programs over two channels from 9:00 a.m. to 9:30 p.m.

Religious Services

Mass, Father J. E. Tupy 9:00
Protestant, Rev. William Anderson 10:00

Movies

December 25 .... "Second Time Around"
December 31-January 1 .... "The Boys' Night Out"

Menu

Christmas Dinner

CELERY STICKS   CRANBERRY SAUCE

ROAST YOUNG TOM TURKEY

CHESTNUT DRESSING

GIBLET GRAVY

FIESTA SALAD   STUFFED OLIVES

SNOWFLAKE POTATOES   CANDIED FRESH YAMS

BUTTERED ASPARAGUS

PARKERHOUSE ROLLS

BREAD & BUTTER

PUMPKIN PIE   FRUIT CAKE

COFFEE WITH CREAM

ALCATRAZ ISLAND

he discovered the man had witnessed weeks of nightly rioting on The Rock and quit the prison service. Dollison remained at Alcatraz for nine years. He soon realized that many men had been transferred against their will. Phil Bergen felt he transferred because he scored well on an exam for lieutenantcy, yet the warden of Lewisburg, where Bergen was a junior officer, didn't like him. The warden wrote on his file "not suitable for promotion," Bergen said. He was given a choice of going to Alcatraz or sticking around. He chose Alcatraz. He retired eventually as associate warden.

Other stories were common of men who had transferred after courting disfavor at other institutions.

Drinking problems, hints of marital impropriety, petty cash scandals, rumors; the prison service is a fairly insulated society, conservative, and in the business of meting out punishment. It was part of the gallows humor on Alcatraz—the occasional story of the prison officer waking up from an all-night drunk and finding himself on a plane to San Francisco.

Turnover was high for other reasons. A Bureau report in 1957 stated that a "general handyman and trash collector [having] no contact with prisoners, earns $300 [more than] the annual salary [for] Correctional Officers." In the same report, a note at the bottom stated, "In one week five at Alcatraz resigned, each giving as his reason that he had been offered more remunerative employment. . . ."

Losing five posts in a week could be devastating for a short-staffed, high-profile prison like Alcatraz.

Moreover, my father casually observed that at times one-third of the officers had less than a year's experience in prison work. "They were as green as grass," Bergen once said, agreeing, "and the prisoners have hundreds of years of experience."

Formal training of Alcatraz officers lasted four weeks, but 95 percent of it consisted of on-the-job advice from senior officers. Although classes of eight or ten men were periodically held, every class experienced several dropouts, and their eventual replacements *only* received on-the-job training. (The inmate, of course, could offer a little advice to the new man.) Alcatraz was so consistently short-staffed that captains took what they could get. "Recruitment was the most serious problem," said Bergen. "Retention was the next."

And what developed over the years, broadly speaking, was two types of employees: those who had remained for many years, gaining their experience primarily at Alcatraz, and those who were new recruits with no prior prison experience. Viewed from a larger perspective, the result caused two dissimilar attitudes which converged to play an eventual part in the demise of Alcatraz. The more experienced officers, who'd been there for a decade or more, believed the prison to be as escape proof as possible, for the observable reason that no one had escaped and resurfaced. They were over-confident in the myth and therefore less conscientious. The less experienced officers, on the other hand, hired quickly and often trained haphazardly, were cynical. They could see the deterioration in the buildings, they felt inadequately trained, and they too were less conscientious. Both groups sloughed off assignments, particularly cell searches and magazine censorship. (Officers let slip through a March 1962 *Popular Science* issue with an article on watertight sailing jackets, and a May 1962 *Sports Illustrated* issue with photographs and description of a rubberized boat from which Morris and the Anglins drew information for their escape attempt. The night of that escape, they only superficially checked noises coming from the cell house roof and they alerted no one.)

Officers and inmates were usually respectful to one another.
(NATIONAL MARITIME MUSEUM; BETTY WALLER COLLECTION)

To an outside observer, it might seem like the entire security system was at risk.

But that's to lay blame for what followed on the guard force, and it's not that simple. Alcatraz was an old, controversial prison, which by the early 1960s was an embarrassment to the Kennedy "New Frontier." Bureau of Prisons' Director James V. Bennett had already abandoned it in his reports to Congress. While he had defended it at budget time nearly every year for 25 years, and sometimes loudly heralded its purpose in the federal prison system, now in 1961 he admitted that it was decrepit, poorly thought-out, and a relic of the past.

By then of course, the island's replacement—the U. S. Prison at Marion, Illinois—was already being built.

In 1961 Olin G. Blackwell became warden and appointed his staff. Bill Bradley became captain of the guards. In a move that astonished many officers, Blackwell appointed Arthur M. Dollison as associate warden. Dollison was considered a businessman. He had served there for eight years, but all of it in industries, and the last year as superintendent of industries. He was a business man, not a custodial officer.

Like the lyrics of a song that would become popular later in the decade, "The times they are a'changin'."

An officer stands on Broadway, his reflection shining on the cleaned and polished concrete floor. (PHIL DOLLISON)

7
The Departure

The concrete floor in the prison cell house today is dull and flat, but when my father accepted the promotion as associate warden the cement was shiny and bright, the result of years of daily cleaning and polish. It was something appreciated by everyone, and a source of pride to prison officers, who pointed to the floors as proof of a well-run institution.

But the sheen was a mirror of sorts, and a tiny crack appeared.

Since Alcatraz closed in 1963, people's stories of what caused its demise have varied . . . one man suggested that during a renovation in the late 1950s, when hot water spigots were plumbed into the cells, a prisoner/maintenance man dropped a star drill, which later a convict found . . . others blame the hanging blankets that mysteriously never made it into the reports . . . others claim a vital tower was shut down on orders from Washington which allowed it to happen . . . a former prisoner fighting for some immortality or integrity, or both, has as much said *he* shut Alcatraz down, solely by supplying the major items used in the 1962 Morris-Anglin escape attempt—the event that closed the prison.

Whatever contributors, the plan could have never worked without the participation of those dust free, shiny, concrete floors.

By June 1962 Blackwell had settled in as warden. He was perhaps the most progressive and colorful senior administrator.

The first warden, Johnston, had directed the conversion of the prison from Army to federal jurisdiction, and served nearly 14 years as the chief gatekeeper. He was a man of the times; more a banker than a prison administrator. He knew prisons only through the front office, and like James V. Bennett, the Bureau director, his actual cell house experience was limited.

His successor, Swope, a difficult, uneasy man, came into the federal service as an appointee from a state prison. Swope was not the spokesman that Johnston was, nor had he the experience that Paul Madigan had. Madigan, the third warden, was the man most prepared for his position; he had come up through the custodial ranks, first as officer, then captain, associate and finally warden. Madigan then named Blackwell his successor. Almost three decades passed between the first and last wardens on Alcatraz, a time of great change in American history.

Blackwell was a tall, rangy Texan with a languid, measured style. The Mexican-American prisoners at La Tuna, Texas, his first prison in the early 1940s, dubbed him "Lagartija," the lizard, and the name fit. He smoked heavily, liked to fish and shoot guns, and had a penchant for lolling out southern expressions. He could talk about someone being "meaner'n'a red dog," or someone having to "hunker down," idioms usually accompanied by a crack in his voice that suggested playfulness.

He remained at the medium security La Tuna institution for 10 years and subsequently was promoted to federal jail inspector supervising a five-and-one-half state territory. "Hasn't anybody ever had to eat one of them damn things?" he once asked

Olin G. Blackwell, Alcatraz warden from 1961 until mid-1963.

a state prison guard who carried a billy club. (Billy clubs, saps, and gas billies were common in prison for many years. Although Johnston claimed he did away with them, their use at Alcatraz was obvious and tolerated. When my father arrived in the mid-1950s they were still in use, and used even on some occasions by the then associate warden. By the last years of Madigan and Blackwell, they were abandoned altogether.) "Blackie" served six years, first as captain of the guards and then associate warden at Lewisburg Penitentiary. He was transferred to Alcatraz and made warden in November 1961, at 46 one of the youngest wardens in the federal system.

Blackwell's humor and casual style earned him many friends in the prison service. "I've had an awful lot of people tell me they were going to kill me if they got a chance," he said once with a twinkle in his eye. "I told some that they'd have to get in line—a lot of people ahead of 'em." But just as quickly he was accused of playing favorites, and actively disliked by some of his staff. He was a hard drinker and island rumors focused on this and other shortcomings. But the real problem for everyone was his goal to relax the atmosphere at Alcatraz. Blackwell was at the cutting edge of a new era. It wasn't the 1930s any longer. But relaxing the prison yet maintaining the vigil put him squarely between the younger more informal guards and the older more experienced ones. Arguably, this allowed for considerable interpretation among both groups.

Moreover, the last years on Alcatraz were not easy. Blackwell inherited a decrepit facility with a poor reputation and little money. The old diesel power plant was giving way and there would be blackouts in the remaining months. The water pipes were disintegrating but not repaired for fear they would crumble altogether. Even the prison building was in need of structural repair. The BOP had spent $300,000 in 1960-61 and an engineering report in 1961 indicated that an additional $4 million would be needed to put The Rock in shape.

While Blackwell was associate warden Hollywood began making *The Birdman of Alcatraz,* starring Burt Lancaster, which added to the pressure. (The film was released while Blackwell was warden. Robert Stroud had already been transferred from Alcatraz by then, partly because he was old, in failing health, and the Bureau of Prisons realized that his death on Alcatraz might cause them some embarassment. He was residing in population at the medical prison in Springfield, Missouri. The public, however, was not informed of that fact and renewed their interest in his release. Stroud died four months after Alcatraz closed in 1963. He had a heart attack at age 71, the day before John F. Kennedy was killed.) "Oh, that actor," Blackwell grumbled, years later:

> *He got mad as hell because I wouldn't let them come on the island and shoot. I was in favor of paroling Stroud to him, you know, let him live with the son-of-a-bitch for a while.*

Blackie was not bothered by "little bitty" escape details. Twenty years after Alcatraz closed, he answered questions with generalities most of the time, refusing to specify, elaborate or illuminate on what had occurred that last year.

But during his reign, censorship of the mail relaxed, as did the working relationships between officers and prisoners. New men liked the new informality, the older guards hated it. Then, after two escape attempts that year, the blame and criticism flew. Blackwell skirted most of the ultimate blame and remained seemingly unconcerned about unanswered questions. "The escapes that happen in any year in any institution are from human failure, nothin' more," he said emphatically. "And I can spell that out for you in exaggerated detail:

> *You can take the so-called 'escape-proof' jail—and they never built one— and I maintain if you put a man in it [he] can get out of it. They're as smart as we are so they can figure a way out. On the other hand, I can take two*

The cell house was built by military convicts from 1908 to 1912. Although it was remodeled in 1934, the corrosion on metal and concrete from the salt sea air was obvious by the 1950s.

*men with shotguns and a hundred inmates in an open field and keep those
people there until they starve to death or they run and I shoot 'em, and I
have maintained security. Haven't lost a prisoner. So. An exaggerated example. No escape has ever been made without human failure.*

Blackwell, however, was unable to see a correlation between the relaxation he
sought and the two escape attempts that year. If his policies were admirable in the
changing world, their execution by his employees was flawed.

The warden hadn't had a vacation in 18 months when he finally left the prison,
with Washington's approval, for a week of fishing that June. My father became the
acting warden.

On Tuesday, June 12, 1962, Acting Lieutenant Bill Long was up in the cell house,
ready to add up the morning count. Suddenly another officer rounded the corner of
B block and said hurriedly, "'Bill, I got one I can't get awake.'" Long's booming voice
rose and fell excitedly:

*And I said, 'Well, hell, I'll get him awake.' I walked up to the cell and I
says, 'Wake up!' and . . . I reached in to tap him on the head and it felt like
it crumbled. I immediately slapped at the head and it rolled on the floor!*

The island phone in our house jangled at 7:20 a.m. with an early morning urgency.
My father reached for it with some dread; it could not be good news.

"Mr. Dollison," the Control Room officer said to the acting warden, "We just found
three dummies up in the cell house."

Dollison was a significant departure from past associate wardens and a clue as to
how the federal prison system was changing. While some had carried billy clubs and
wore their SOB reputations proudly, my father was a quiet-spoken, careful man.

He had been college-educated, but like many men his age, had applied for the job
in the prison service during the depression. He was tall and thin, and five pounds
too light, but they gave him a week to pass the physical. He didn't gain an ounce, but
on the day of the physical he bought six pounds of bananas, sat down by a railroad
track, and ate them all. He hated bananas after that, but he got the job.

It was typical of his determination and stoicism. He was a quiet man, unpreten-
tious and practical, but distant by the time we could talk. (I remember as a child
sitting on his lap while he read the comics to me, but that was before Alcatraz.) He
seldom waffled, and stood his ground once he made up his mind.

To understand my father, I always felt, was to understand prison men—his conservative footing tempered by a desire to help, his cynicism tethered by enthusiasm—remarkable given the maximum security setting.

His most over-riding trait was his morality, which, when coupled with a calm exterior, made him seem conservative and less exciting perhaps than other men, but he often surprised me by his liberal attitudes. Although he found it difficult to believe most prisoners' stories, once, on a hunch that a prisoner was being framed when an escape note was found in his cell, he took the note and other samples of the man's writing to a San Francisco handwriting expert. The results were inconclusive, but he backed the prisoner.

He was perhaps driven as much by curiosity as convinced of the man's innocence, because inquisitiveness was a basic trait. He was an assiduous reader, with a sharpened sense of history. Learning was a lifelong pursuit. Thus it was difficult for him to understand those who lacked interest or whose logic was faulty. I can still remember with some trauma the fingernails of his thick, padded hands drumming the table as he doggedly explained mathematics to me. He had undeniable patience, but he could harden with an imposing, acerbic authority when practice didn't make perfect. He seldom swore in anger, never raised his voice, yet his fingers made those table points.

Over the years he transferred from Leavenworth to the federal prison in Ashland, Kentucky, then after a hiatus in the Army he returned and eventually transferred to the federal prison in Terre Haute, Indiana. There he moved over to industries. He had white hair by then, and his cobalt-blue eyes seemed a little narrower. He worked nights for four years to complete a correspondence course in accounting when he transferred to Alcatraz.

He seldom talked about work, and at Alcatraz, this became more pronounced.   I learned over the years, however, that the human condition, especially as represented in prison, was a source of drollery to him. He thought prisoners devoted a lot of time trying to convince themselves and each other that they were innocent, when he mostly felt otherwise. One of his stories concerned a prisoner serving a life sentence for kidnapping. For years the man submitted writs to obtain a new trial. When in fact he did get a retrial, he spent considerable time

Arthur M. Dollison, associate warden on Alcatraz from 1961 until November 1962. (PHIL DOLLISON)

among his inmate friends talking up his prowess as a writ-writer and gloating over his possible release. This did not endear him to many cons, and worse, he was eventually foiled.

In a retrial he charged the woman kidnap victim with complicity, and counted on witnesses forgetting details in the nine years he'd been in prison. Despite that, he was found guilty, and more horrifying, he was given the death sentence. His sentence was at the last minute reduced to life imprisonment but it did little to salve his ego, because his new sentence voided his already served nine years, and he had to start all over again. Instead of returning to Alcatraz a hero, he became the butt of jokes.

My father's stories were not gleeful. One could easily see the wry chuckle and cocked eyebrow as amused interpreters of the foibles within us all. Nonetheless, somewhere along the line, he had taken on the callousness of prison work. A small detail perhaps, in a prison mural replete with them.

Transferring to industries was logical because he was clearly a businessman more accustomed to organizing numbers than guarding people. As superintendent, he reorganized Alcatraz industries, raising the pay rate for prisoners and changing some shops from an hourly scale to a piece-rate scale—thereby increasing incentive and production.

Blackwell picked Dollison as associate warden because of this innovation and because he knew most prisoners better than a new man would. But Dad was not a custodial man. He had little experience on the tiers. "We knew the Bureau was falling apart then," one officer joked later, adding that today the prison service has changed so much even ministers have become wardens.

But all this was oblivious to me in 1961 when Dad walked into my room and asked how I'd feel if we moved back to Alcatraz. A sense of excitement overtook me. I was 14 and in my first year of high school. I quickly realized that we'd have to leave my dog behind, that I'd have to transfer schools and make new friends, that there'd be the boat again, the sometimes miserable weather, the restriction and curfews. But ever since we'd moved off the island when I was about nine years old I'd always wanted to go back. Part of it, I knew, was the sense of notoriety that I enjoyed. (Well-meaning friends used to embarass me by blurting out, "Meet my friend. She *lives* on *Alcatraz.*") But looking back now I realize it was also the sense of adventure I saw coming. I didn't know what adventure I imagined, until the phone rang that June morning in 1962.

Dad had been associate warden of the nation's most maximum security penitentiary for seven months by then. Despite the man I thought I understood, even he was controversial. "Your dad, when he was associate warden," said Bob Fawson, one of the younger guards on the island at the time, "was a very hard man." But Marvin Orr, one of the older guards, once said, "I don't think your father was quite tough enough." Now, with the warden gone for the week, Dad was acting warden. "Take Art there," said Officer Fred Mahan, "he was just learning the ropes. . ."

By the time Dollison and Bradley got to the cell house that morning, officers had determined that Frank Lee Morris and John and Clarence Anglin had crawled out vents in the back of their cells the night before, then shimmied up the utility pipes to a vent in the roof.

Frank Lee Morris, #AZ 1441, was a 35-year-old with a tested IQ of 135; he was a 5'7", bantam weight, stern-faced, disciplined Southerner. Records showed he had a devil's head tatooed on his right arm. Morris had been shuffled from one foster home to another since he was one year old.

He was first caught violating the law at age 13. A series of petty larcenies, house break-ins, burglaries, armed robberies, narcotics violations, parole violations and escapes had led him from boys training school to jail to prison. He served time in Washington, D.C., Ohio, Louisiana, Florida, and Alabama, until he wound up at Atlanta Federal Penitentiary in Georgia on a sentence of 14 years for a bank heist.

The San Francisco newspapers that June made much of the fact that he was seemingly intelligent. But he was caught once burglarizing a Louisiana bank, which netted him only $6,165—not a large sum of money even in the 1950s. But worse, the booty—in coins—weighed 1200 pounds.

Numerous escape attempts at Florida State Pen, sawing through bars in a Louisiana solitary cell, and an attempted escape from Atlanta, all convinced federal authorities that Alcatraz should be his home. Morris had arrived in January 1960.

John Anglin, #AZ 1476, at 32, was a year older than his brown-haired, hot-headed brother, Clarence, #AZ 1485. Both were taller than Morris, at nearly six feet. They were serving 10 and 17 years respectively for bank robbery. The Anglins were loud-mouthed. Some officers felt that if they hadn't had someone in control over them the entire institution would have known about the plot in two weeks.

They had previous escape attempts on record but none as complex as this. The most ambitious occurred at Leavenworth in the late 1950s when Clarence was found hiding in a large bread box destined for outside the gate. It was a lame attempt which eventually got him to Alcatraz.

That morning, officers placed Allen C. West in segregation after he reportedly stated, "You may as well lock me up too. I planned the entire escape."

West, #AZ 1335, a short, dark-haired, wiry 33-year-old inmate, serving a ten-year sentence for interstate transportation of stolen vehicles, was described as a "go-fer" by one guard and a manipulator by several others. He had been at Alcatraz twice, in 1954-56 and again in 1958-63. During his second stint in October 1960 he and several prisoners in D block had cut their heel tendons. This is considered by officers to be an old prison ploy to attract attention, usually on mental harassment claims, or to get out of work. West's wounds were said to be superficial and later he claimed he'd been badgered into doing it. He was assigned to cell house maintenance after getting out of D block in May 1961—more than a year before the actual "unauthorized departure," and that was when he began thinking about escaping.

Alcatraz had been an old military prison—prisoners could see the deterioration in the building as well as anyone; cracks appeared frequently and cornices fell off—but it was doubtful West knew that the heating vents behind the cells had been made smaller when the feds took over in 1934. And it wasn't even known by officials that work crews hadn't reinforced the cement around the vents with steel rods or wire mesh, but the erosion was visible.

The heating vents had at one time been larger. (NATIONAL MARITIME MUSEUM)

West brought John Anglin in on the deal first, he told Dollison and Captain Bradley—they had been acquaintances at Florida Penitentiary—then brought Morris in.

According to prison and FBI reports of items found in the prisoners' cells, the quartet used hack saw blades, scraps of serrrated tin, six-inch homemade chisels with taped handles, and table utensils with sharpened edges. Some officers thought the convicts used star drills which they had found after replumbing the cell house, but no such drills were listed in the reports.

They worked at night, beginning in December 1961, digging first one hole, then another, until they had 20 or 30 and could chip away large chunks of the cement. To hide the larger and larger holes, Clarence Anglin made fake cardboard ventilator grills with simulated concrete to fit over the enlarged vents. Towels hanging down from their sinks also hid the openings.

Clarence also made dummy heads. The papier mache

half-heads were covered in a heavy soap-like material that enabled the facial features to be easily molded and painted in flesh tones. They were complete even to the detail of an ear and topped off with human hair probably obtained from the barber shop. When two masks and two grills were finished, two men could climb out of their cells, replace the grills and work atop the cell block. West had convinced a cell house officer—or got another prisoner to convince the officer—to put blankets around the top of the cell block. Now they could work on the ceiling ventilators.

Up there, they began making life jackets. Later FBI examination of a homemade life preserver left atop the cell block showed incredible ingenuity. Using raincoats, they not only sewed the seams but used hot steam pipes to vulcanize them, making them—they hoped—airtight. They also used spray bottle tops to inflate the jackets. West admitted getting the ideas from the magazines that slipped through the censors.

It was obvious that many other prisoners supplied materials. Besides paste, soap, paint, and human hair, reports showed they also used tools, a vacuum motor, heavy denim cloth, 50 or 60 raincoats, cardboard, piping, a homemade flashlight with batteries, pieces of quarter-inch scrap metal, iron wire, rods, wooden paddles made in industries, and names and addresses of friends and relatives.

But prisoners interviewed in the next days said they knew nothing of the escape, either before or that night. According to official memos prisoner #1294 said he was playing his violin, heard nothing, knew nothing and had no idea anything was going on. (Officers reported later that the musicians in the population were told that night to play more quietly.) Prisoner #1415 said no one asked him for any help and even if he did know anything, he would not tell administration. Prisoner #1329 said he knew nothing, heard no noises that night, claimed he was reading and can"really get lost when I am reading a book." About 28 prisoners were questioned. "You know I'm not going to talk about that," was one comment reported, "it's worth my life."

Two other prisoners were also found to have holes drilled around their vents, one with 31 holes. Both denied involvement, and one said he would take a lie detector test if it were given by someone not connected with the U.S. government.

According to both FBI and prison reports, West claimed they built a 6' by 14' raft out of prison raincoats, with 15-inch pontoons around the edge and underneath, as well as four life preservers. If they built a pontoon raft, it was a second raft; another, a partially completed rubber raft approximately 6' by 2' with a wooden valve, was left behind on top of cell block B. West said they inflated the raincoat raft they had taken with a musical instrument called a concertina.

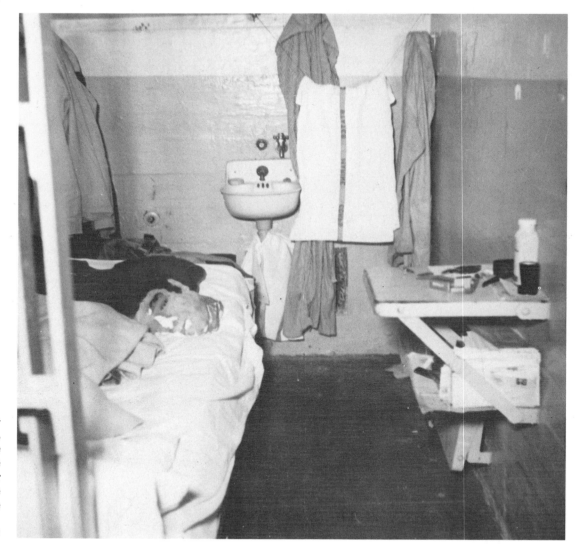

The masks made by Clarence Anglin were quite life-like. This photo, taken on June 12, shows one on the bed and towels hanging from the sink which concealed the ventilator opening to the utility corridor. Once in the corridor, the men climbed the pipes to the cell house roof.

(NATIONAL MARITIME MUSEUM)

The three slipped out Monday, June 11, at about 9:30 p.m.

West never saw them again. He claimed his fake grill had been cemented so tight he was unable to loosen it that night, but he repeatedly acknowledged fear of the water.

He told Dollison, Bradley and later Blackwell and the FBI agents that Morris had planned to go north to Angel Island, eventually to Marin County, where they were to have robbed a hardware store for guns, clothes and money, then stolen a helicopter for a planned getaway to a desert somewhere. Morris had read about helicopters and thought he could pilot one. They had also discussed digging a hole in the desert big enough to hide a truck, where they would hide for a month until the heat wore off.

Such a plan, my father commented wearily later that night, would have left a trail as thick as blood.

"Good Lord!" said Jean Long to my mother and me that Tuesday morning when she came to our house. "Billy was on the parade ground until 9:30 last night."

A shudder went up my spine when I thought of it. It had been a balmy evening June 11th when the trio left their cells and climbed down the roof to the shoreline. A group of us had played a late game of baseball on the parade ground.

I had awakened the next morning to the unfamiliar sound of the escape siren, and mother and I had searched the house and basement. The island was still; for a while it seemed like a ghost town.

Jean Long crept along #64 building trying to get back to her apartment, she told me later. She remembered the stillness being punctured by fright when she rounded the corner of the building and ran headlong into a man. "Scared the you-know-what out of both of us!" she said, laughing.

LuAnne Freeman worked on the mainland that Tuesday, where she could see Alcatraz from her window. "I was sitting at my desk and the mailman came through and said, 'Some of your neighbors took off this morning,' and I said, 'Sure they did.' I assumed he was talking about San Quentin. But he said, 'Call out there and see.' Well I finally got the island. I threatened to swim if they didn't send the boat for me. I wanted to know where the kids were!"

"My wife was working at the time and the kids hadn't left for school yet. I was worried about them," said Fred Freeman, who'd already been assigned up top:

The first chance I got I called down to the house and told them to go next door. I didn't have time to worry. When they told me they were all right I knew the inmates hadn't been at the house.

Doreen and Mike Pitzer had been driving from McNeil Island, Washington, with their parents when they arrived on Alcatraz in the midst of the crisis that Tuesday. Their father had just been transferred from the medium security institution where they'd grown up. "We couldn't have arrived on a worse day!" Doreen said:

We got off the boat and walked to the waiting room. Billy Rogers was hanging over the balcony of #64 building, looking [at us]. Remember how the kids used to scope out the other kids?! [She laughed.] I remember clearly, they had bloodhounds on the dock—maybe three of them. I remember that baying. I'd never seen bloodhounds until then. I kept thinking, 'I don't know about this!'

"My kid and I were out fishing in Lake Berryessa," Warden Blackwell said many years later, "and I saw this boat comin' straight at us across the lake:

And I says, 'Uh-oh, we got problems' and the kid could see that too, and we started reelin' in and puttin' our gear together. And sure enough the man that run the boat dock pulled up and said, 'I don't know what the problem is but they want you to call Alcatraz right away.'

"As soon as they hollered for me," said Officer Virgil Cullen later, "I ran up there and asked Capt. Bradley, "What happened, they go out the top?" Bradley was a stocky, friendly man who'd been on Alcatraz just a short time from Leavenworth Penitentiary. He was said to have commented many times on his skepticism of Alcatraz' reputation for housing the nation's worst prisoners. Although he was well-liked—not always good in a captain of the guards—and respected by some of his officers, others thought he didn't run a tight enough operation. The question had to have been a disconcerting one for Bradley.
"And he says, 'Yeah, how'd you know?' "
"And I said, 'Them damn mattress covers.' He just looked at me and grinned:

I had been working the day or so before that, and I jumped on the lieutenant about putting blankets all around the top of the cell house. I asked him why, because I could not see the inmate working up there. He said, 'That's

all right. They're painting up there and I don't want the paint to come down-
stairs.' I'd say there were maybe 30-40 blankets up there.

Despite the fantastic attention to detail by West, Morris and the Anglin brothers, this escape attempt would have been impossible without a corresponding number of oversights by officers and administrators.

The officer supervising West locked him into the utility corridor without direct control; this was a minor security breach at Alcatraz and rested heavily on the prevalent feeling that the island was an "escape proof" bastion, and that West could do no harm in there.

Secondly, each of the four cells had been shaken down in April and again in June without detection of the fake grill panels or significant contraband. Moreover, the night of the escape, officers heard noises that one described as sounding as if some-one had hit an empty five gallon oil drum with the palm of the hand. A preliminary check with the cell house intercom system and a search of the hospital on the second floor of the cell house revealed nothing, and the officer returned to the Control Center to make out his report. The report did not state that he checked outside the building, or alerted the tower officers, however.

It was, of course, the sound of the ventilator cap on the roof being knocked open. In a strict custodial atmosphere such a noise would have initiated a stand-up count. Black-well laid blame on his lieutenants and officers "who go around making security checks and tickin' bars," protest-ing, "and again, the relaxed attitude had nothing to do with that type of performance."

Most importantly, however, at least two officers, a lieu-tenant and a cell-house-in-charge gave in to the argument that blankets hung at the top of the cell block were needed to keep dust and paint chips from falling onto the clean, shiny, concrete floor. (Various prisoners may have aided the ploy by complaining of paint chips falling onto their cell beds.) Because of this major security breach, at least two prisoners were able to leave their cells nightly, over a period of two months, to work atop cell block B, hidden by blankets,

FBI wanted poster of John Anglin.
(ART DOLLISON)

while guards continuously counted their masks.

Blackwell talked about the blankets; every officer and prisoner who was on Alcatraz in 1962 and who was interviewed mentioned the blankets as an obvious component of the attempt. (Estimates varied from a half a dozen hung to 30 or 40.) Yet, in personally signed escape activity reports in my possession, from officers and lieutenants to the captain, from the captain to the associate warden, from the associate warden to the warden, from the warden to the Bureau, the summary report by Bureau of Prisons' Assistant Director Fred T. Wilkinson, as well as the FBI reports, *no mention* was ever made of the blankets. If one were to rely on the reports alone, it would appear as if the blankets never existed.

It seemed, said Wilkinson, who supervised the investigation of the escape attempt, that security at Alcatraz had come to rest on image instead of fact. But that assumes that the Bureau was entirely blameless, which it wasn't.

Clarence Anglin had a talent for making the face masks and fake cardboard grills which hid their activities.

ESCAPED FEDERAL PRISONER

I. O.
No. 3584
6-18-62

WANTED BY FBI
FRANK LEE MORRIS

FBI No. 2,157,606

22 M 9 U 100 12
L 1 U 000

ALIASES: Carl Cecil Clark, Frank Laine, Frank Lane, Frank William Lyons, Frankie Lyons, Stanley O'Neal Singletary, and others

Photographs taken 1960

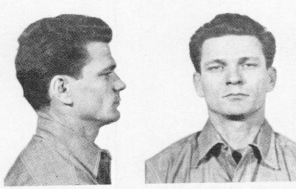

Frank Lee Morris

DESCRIPTION

AGE: 35, born September 1, 1926, Washington, D. C.
HEIGHT: 5' 7½"
WEIGHT: 135 pounds
BUILD: medium
HAIR: brown
EYES: hazel
COMPLEXION: ruddy
RACE: white
NATIONALITY: American
OCCUPATIONS: car salesman, draftsman, painter
SCARS AND MARKS: numerous tattoos including devil's head upper right arm, star base of left thumb, "13" base of left index finger

CRIMINAL RECORD

Morris has been convicted of burglary, larceny of an automobile, grand larceny, possession of narcotics, bank burglary, armed robbery and escape.

CAUTION

MORRIS HAS BEEN REPORTED TO BE ARMED IN THE PAST AND HAS A PREVIOUS RECORD OF ATTEMPTED ESCAPE. CONSIDER EXTREMELY DANGEROUS.

A Federal warrant was issued on June 13, 1962, at San Francisco, California, charging Morris with escaping from the Federal Penitentiary at Alcatraz in violation of Title 18, U.S. Code, Section 751.

IF YOU HAVE INFORMATION CONCERNING THIS PERSON, PLEASE CONTACT YOUR LOCAL FBI OFFICE. PHONE NUMBER LISTED BELOW. OTHER OFFICES LISTED ON BACK.

Identification Order No. 3584
June 18, 1962

J. Edgar Hoover
Director
Federal Bureau of Investigation
Washington 25, D. C.

From the beginning rumors circulated on the island that Alcatraz would close. In 1953 when my father arrived, he was advised not to unpack his furniture. But by the summer of 1962, everyone knew the rumors were true.

(PHIL DOLLISON)

8

The Controversy

Money was the problem.

Alcatraz had always been financially strapped, despite—perhaps because of—its costliness. In January 1962, BOP Director Bennett said that while other institutions needed $5.27 a day per prisoner, Alcatraz needed $13.81. Everything at Alcatraz took more money. While most prisons required $4 per day per prisoner for security, at Alcatraz security cost $9.69. Food costs were higher, transportation was higher, and even water, which had to be barged from the mainland, was an added expense.

Alcatraz business managers sometimes used ingenious methods to make ends meet. One former business manager, who wanted anonymity, combed military surplus property sales for items. One year he purchased the slop chests from 21 ships, thus salvaging enough tooth paste and shaving cream to get Alcatraz through the year.

The paucity of money also hurt the officer corps on Alcatraz, who were largely regarded by the Bureau—in theory as well as practice—as the least important component of the prison, third behind prisoners and administration. "Basically you were assigned to a post with an experienced officer who told you to read the post orders and then ask questions," said one officer. "And that was training. They gave you a big set of keys and said, 'Don't lose 'em.' " Officers learned mostly from good senior officers.

"The brass from Washington weren't interested in the feelings of the guards," George Gregory explained. "They *were* interested in the feelings of the inmates because they wanted to keep them quiet."

Even Blackwell cited a lack of training for employees at Alcatraz because of poor funding. "From the Bureau on down, [they] took the attitude that this was the end of the road," he explained:

People there didn't need anything and wasn't going anyplace. All they needed was to lock them up and throw the key away. That was the atti-

tude, so they didn't devote any money to training. . . . An institution of that type needs a high grade of employee. You take 20-30,000 inmates, skim off the toughest, roughest, meanest, most incorrigible 280 and put 'em in one little bunnel, then you need some top grade people out there.

Blackwell said he didn't think the Bureau tried to direct the day-to-day operations at Alcatraz as it did the other institutions. "They gave the warden a pretty free hand," he admitted, "they may have given us more than we should have had."

Poor funding was also a factor in one other serious matter at Alcatraz that last year. They shut down a tower position.

Originally Alcatraz operated with six towers. The Dock, Road, and Main towers operated 24 hours. The Hill, Model Roof, and Power House towers operated only during daylight hours when prisoners were out of their cells.

To save expenses, and with Washington's approval, Warden Swope closed the Main and Power House sites in the early 1950s. The Main Tower, on top of the cell house, would have been line-of-sight patrol during the 1962 Morris-Anglin escape attempt, but it had long since been abandoned as useless.

That left four towers, only two of which operated 24 hours—the Dock and Road towers. "You couldn't operate the prison without those two," said Bergen emphatically.

But in 1962 Blackwell allegedly closed the Road Tower at night, reducing night surveillance by half.

Washington had approved the dismantling of tower positions in other prisons before, and subsequent escapes were the result, officers have said. It happened at both Lewisburg and Leavenworth. Despite that, and even though Bennett knew the physical plant at Alcatraz was badly deteriorated, the Bureau allowed the elimination of a tower.

"Two Tower—the Road Tower—was not manned at night," said Officer Levinson. "Sure it was crazy . . ." He never knew why it was closed, but he had a theory—like everyone else.

"The Road Tower was shut down during the administration of Blackwell and Bradley," Fawson said emphatically. "It was shut down to conserve personnel. The inmates weren't supposed to know it, but of course they did."

"Number Two Tower was shut down before the Morris-Anglin escape," said Fred Freeman.

"There was a lot of controversy over that deal," said Alcatraz officer Ken Blair.

"Those were quite pertinent to the operations," Blackwell said many years later about the Road Tower and the so-called Kitchen Cage, which was manned particularly when the culinary inmates were out of their cells. Some officers also said that they thought that position was shut down the last months, thus aiding John Paul Scott and Darl Parker in their December 1962 attempt. " I couldn't quite visualize us cutting down on 'em. Maybe we did, I can't say whether we didn't," Blackwell said. When queried as to whether Capt. Bradley had shut down the tower, or had urged him to do so, Blackwell said curtly, "*Bradley* wouldn't have had any authority to close down a tower. *I* could have ordered the closing of a tower, but not *Bradley*."

"Blackie told me he received a letter from Washington," Dollsion said many years after 1962. "I didn't see it . . . I guess they hadn't decided whether to shut down the island or not, and they were still looking for ways to cut down on expense . . . But I remember Blackie talking about it. Before it was shut down. He wanted to know what I thought about it."

When interviewed, Blackwell was asked if Washington had approved in writing the elimination of tower positions.

"No," he said.

[Why do I get reports that tower positions were shut down?]

"I just couldn't tell you. I wouldn't have the slightest idea," he said.

[Did you order their elimination?]

"To my knowledge I did not," he said. "I can't visualize any compensation [for] the shut down of towers, because we needed all the security we could get . . . I have to qualify everything by saying it's been a long time . . . But logic would tell you we would not shut down a tower."

"I can't understand Blackie not—" my father broke off, incredulous. *"Did he say he didn't know anything about it at all?"*

The Bureau of Prisons denied to me all Freedom of Information requests pertaining to correspondence between Alcatraz and the Bureau those last two years. Officers were unsure exactly when the Road Tower went down; some thought it closed before the Morris-Anglin escape attempt: others, including my father, were sure it closed after June 1962: some confused it with the Kitchen Cage position; others thought *both* shut down. One or two claimed to know nothing about it, although everyone was privy to Alcatraz' incessant rumor mill. But all of it only underlined the lack of communication even among the officer-corps on Alcatraz on a very important issue. Some of those who remembered and remarked on it did so with caution. One even cited fear of his government retirement pension being yanked.

Not enough substantive evidence exists to suggest that the Road Tower was shut down before June 1962, although it's troubling that the trio was noisily on the cell house roof just yards from that position. And, if the official version of the Scott-Parker escape route is taken at face value, the Road Tower had no significance in that escape attempt.

But the Kitchen Cage was definitely involved in the Scott-Parker attempt. It was either not manned, or the officer inside it never saw the out-of-pocket prisoners.

I wrote Blackwell finally, concentrating only on the Kitchen Cage. "Did you receive orders from Washington to eliminate it?" I asked. "If so, why?"

Blackwell replied almost immediately. It was a handwritten note on ruled paper, and signed with his confident, flamboyant signature. It said:

> *I have a faint recollection of the so called 'Kitchen Tower' you speak of. The action-dates-escapes-etc.—do not ring a* **positive bell** *with me—so the only thing I can offer—is use the information you have at hand—you seem to be very positive with it. So there is really no need for me to get involved. The very best in your endeavor—Olin G. Blackwell.*

The word "positive" in the phrase "positive bell" was heavily underlined.

Evidence washing up in June 1962 was inconclusive about the Morris-Anglin trio as well. Prison records showed that they hadn't received visitors, and coupled with the prison mail censorship, couldn't have easily made plans for a rendezvous with a boat in the bay.

On June 12, a home-made paddle floating in the bay near Angel Island was retrieved by the Coast Guard and quickly identified as matching one found on cell block B.

On June 15, in the middle of the day, the U.S. Army debris boat, *Coyote,* found an apparently water-proof package in the debris net. It was fished out of the bay also near Angel Island. It contained nine slips of paper with names and addresses, various letters, receipts, and almost 80 photographs of friends and relatives. The contents were sealed inside two plastic bags. It was logical to assume prisoners with few outside contacts would not drop such an item, even to throw off authorities.

On June 21, a man, his wife, and daughter picked up what appeared to be a home-made, olive-drab life preserver off Marin County. It matched ones found atop cell block B. One officer who saw it claimed the yoke-type preserver was still tied, making

Preceding page: The Rock sits in one of the most beautiful and largest bays along the West Coast, with Angel Island and Marin County to the north and the city of San Francisco to the south. The 1962 Morris-Anglin escape attempt was said to have initiated one of the largest manhunts since the Lindbergh baby kidnapping, incorporating the entire shoreline, Angel Island, and all friends and relatives.
(NATIONAL MARITIME MUSEUM)

This page: Alcatraz prisoners leave the prison yard.
(COURTESY OF PHIL DOLLISON)

it appear that the prisoner had passed out and drowned—his body slipping out later.

On June 22, an Alcatraz boat operator found another home-made, olive-drab life preserver located about 50 yards east of Alcatraz.

No 6' by 14' raft was ever found—a rather large item, whether inflated or not, to haul around. The concertina alleged to have been used to inflate it was also not found. It appears that West lied about the raft, particularly because the smaller raft was still atop cell block B. No bodies surfaced; no robberies occurred, especially of hardware or gun shops, to implicate the trio; they simply vanished without a trace. The FBI staked out all family members, former friends, and what few correspondents they had. Nothing turned up. Federal warrents were issued, and bonds set at $50,000 each were lodged. FBI records stated that a transcription of leads would produce "some 100 pages of negative information and then serve no useful purpose."

Finally, anyone reviewing the prisoners' record would easily ascertain that these three had life-long criminal histories which netted them nothing more than jails and prisons. They weren't good at staying clean. Particularly in this instance, they needed to rob to get money and clothing. They would have had to pay off anyone who ever saw or aided them.

It was presumed logically by most—but not all—that they drowned that night.

West transferred off Alcatraz in January 1963, then was released from federal custody at Atlanta in January '65. In 1969 he was received by the Florida Department of Corrections on charges of grand larceny, robbery and attempted escape. With his long record and two Alcatraz terms, he was sentenced to one commitment for five years, one for life, and one for three years, to run concurrent. In 1978, when he was 48 years old, he died in prison of unspecified "natural causes."

The event, of course, closed the prison, but it was little more than a foregone conclusion anyway. Clearly more than just physical deterioration brought down the old, unpopular, coarseback penitentiary. In fact, what had occurred was a confluence of poor public reputation, media-generated myth, and neglect, erosion and incompetence that began at the very top. Ultimately, the Bureau of Prisons was responsible. From Bennett down, security had lapsed: lack of funding, lack of training, using Alcatraz as a threat to officers in other institutions, eliminating key security positions, allowing the most high profile, high security penitentiary to be short staffed, all contributed to the ignominious ending of an institution which, ironically, despite public disfavor and governmental neglect, operated for most of its years as professionally as any prison in the United States.

The first 32 prisoners on Alcatraz were transfers from the Army prison. The last prisoner assigned a number—who arrived December 20, 1962—was Az #1576.

The Bureau of Prisons did, however, lay blame in an ineffectual and inequitable attempt to show its concern. Two officers, who counted dummies numerous times on two shifts were suspended without pay for 30 days. Many officers agreed that the dummies were so life-like they too would have counted them. And Capt. Bradley was leveled with "a high degree of responsibility for the ineffectiveness of inspections, patrols and security measures. . ."

Associate Warden Dollison was not given official reprimand, but transferred to one of the most minimum security institutions in the federal system, Seagoville Federal Correctional Institution, the last days of 1962. It was an unofficial way to show disfavor.

Official reprimands were not leveled against the cell house lieutenants who permitted the blankets to remain in plain view above cell block B, because the blankets were not acknowledged in the official reports. Nor were the evening shift officers reprimanded for their cursory checks of cell house noises the night of the Morris-Anglin escape attempt. Blackwell was not cited for his lack of leadership. And of course, no report cited the Bureau for its ultimate responsibility. To educate its own enormous staff throughout the country on the anatomy of an escape attempt and detail its own involvement was too much to ask. A full investigation—without reprimand to anyone—would have uncovered more of the actual causes leading to the escape attempt, and perhaps furthered the Bureau of Prisons in its projected image as a professional example to the world.

It was originally decided to close Alcatraz in December 1963, but the date was hastily moved up when Scott and Parker slipped through the cracks in December '62. And worse, Blackwell wrote my father in January 1963 that in the last days an ex-con forged a court order that almost got another Alcatraz prisoner off the island. The discovery was a lucky break for the chief gatekeeper, Blackwell, who'd had two too many infamous escape attempts from Alcatraz that year.

Then, on March 21, 1963, the last prisoners were escorted off The Rock. A few weeks later Blackwell left for Lewisburg, Pennsylvania, as warden.

Justice Department officials had told reporters in 1934 when the penitentiary opened as the maximum security citadel, "We are looking forward to great things from Alcatraz." I am not sure what the attorney general meant when he issued the statement, and within what context it was said, or whether it was even correctly quoted in the newspapers. But among those great things were a toweringly expensive, fatally deteriorated prison, and a concept of security that began in myth and ended in misfortune.

Epilogue

Although the last handful of prisoners left The Rock on March 21, 1963, it officially closed in June. Except for a caretaker and his wife, John and Marie Hart, the island remained largely vacant. Then in March 1964, again in early November 1969, and finally on November 20, 1969, "Indians of all Tribes" occupied Alcatraz and claimed it as their own. The last well-publicized occupation lasted nearly 19 months before government agents escorted them off the island.

It was estimated that thousands of people landed on Alcatraz during the years it was abandoned, causing irreparable damage. The warden's residence, the officers' clubhouse, and the lighthouse residence were all destroyed by fire, and many other parts of the island were subject to wanton destruction and pilfering. The government then destroyed other buildings—the associate warden's/captain's residence and apartment buildings A,B, and C—to thwart other attempted occupations.

Alcatraz became a hot topic in the years 1969-1970, when one private financier tried to buy it to build an amusement park, and other people advanced other ideas. Finally in 1972 Alcatraz became a part of the Golden Gate National Recreation Area, as part of the National Parks.

Notes

Chapter 3
page 19:
Notes were gleaned from notebooks kept by several officers who allowed me to see them and from my father's collection of notes written during inmate classification meetings he attended at Alcatraz.
page 33:
Letters are a part of 25-30 letters my father kept in his private papers, written by prisoners usually asking to go back to work after a fight with another inmate had occurred.
page 42:
Studies dealing with prison officers are almost unanimous in expressing the difficult position of the prison officer, the "man in the middle," who feels pressure from administrators to maintain a high degree of security, and pressure from prisoners to relax the constant vigilence. It is commonly understood that prison officers often feel that they too are in "in for life."

Chapter 6
page 91:
Turnover among prison guards has always been one of the most perplexing problems facing prisons. Generally state and federal prisons are located in rural areas and draw employees from these areas. Despite the fact that the job offers benefits such as retirement, it is by comparison low paying and often largely unrewarding, especially initially. Many people, also, are unprepared for the tension and potential violence.

Chapter 7:
Information on the Morris-Anglin escape attempt was gleaned from Freedom of Information requests to the FBI; Bureau of Prisons' reports; Alcatraz memos from officers, lieutenants, the captain, the associate warden, the assistant director of the Bureau, and interviews with prisoners taken just after the escape attempt among Arthur Dollison's private papers; news stories from *The San Francisco Chronicle* and *The San Francisco Examiner;* interviews with officers and administrators, and my own observations. The information on the blankets and the towers was uncovered through interviews.

Chapter 8
page 119: The existence of an escape raft was never clearly determined. It has always been my suspicion that it didn't exist, or else sank quickly, leaving the three would-be escapists to flounder in the cold, choppy waters.
page 119:
My father reported that a foreign freighter spotted a body tentatively identified as one with clothing similar to an Alcatraz prisoner, floating in the ocean just outside the Gate about a week after the incident. Because the captain allegedly had no radio contact, he didn't report the sighting until too late to pick up the remains. Although my father related the incident to the FBI, it did not make it into the subsequent reports in my possession.

Index

Photographs are italicised.